How to Teach Reading When You're Not a Reading Teacher

Revised Edition

⊞

By Dr. Sharon H. Faber

Incentive Publications, Inc.
Nashville, Tennessee

"If I'd a knowed what a trouble it is
to make a book I wouldn't a tackled it
and ain't a goin' to no more."
— *Mark Twain*

Acknowledgment

For all their unconditional love and support, I want to thank:

my mother, Nelda Strong,
who has always been my role model, inspiration,
and the best mom a girl could have;

my children, Robert and Julie,
who are the pride and joy of my life;

and my husband, Conrad,
who is my soul mate, best friend, and the love of my life.

Illustrated by Marta J. Drayton
Cover by Rebecca Rüegger
Edited by Jill Norris
Copyedited by Cary Grayson

ISBN 978-0-86530-000-2
Library of Congress Control Number 2007934311

7 8 9 10   13 12

Printed by Sheridan Books, Inc., Chelsea, Michigan • August 2012
www.incentivepublications.com

TABLE OF CONTENTS

INTRODUCTION

Reading is probably the most difficult task
we ask the brain to undertake.

— *David Sousa*

A Personal Note

I was not trained as a reading teacher. I was an English major who became an English teacher. Being a teacher was something I wanted to do since I was a little girl. (I had four younger brothers who let me "pretend" that I was their teacher.) After graduating from college, my plan was simple: I wanted to teach the subject I loved and instill that same love into the hearts and minds of all my students. I dreamed of making the classic books, plays, and poetry come alive for them as they always had for me. I was going to share my passion and inspire students to love and appreciate literature as part of their lives.

When I finally became a "real" teacher, I had the biggest shock of my life. Not only were many of my students unenthusiastic about both school and my English class, but some of them couldn't even read! It had never occurred to me that I would get students who would be struggling readers or even non-readers. I thought that all children learned to read in kindergarten and first grade—at least by they time they were out of elementary school! How could I be getting kids this age who couldn't even read? I was trained to be an English teacher; I wasn't trained to be a reading teacher.

Even worse, I found that some students could "read" and pronounce the words in their assignments, but when we discussed the content, it was as if they had never done the reading. It was painfully clear to me that some of my so-called "best" readers were only "word-callers"! They could recognize the words, but they struggled (or failed) to extract meaning from what they had read.

I had some serious questions:

- *How could I teach students to appreciate literary content when they couldn't read even a short story or a simple poem—let alone an entire book?*

- *What could I do to help these students develop the reading skills they needed in order to deal with life?*

This book is a compilation of the ideas and strategies collected from many sources over many years, organized in a way that busy teachers will find useful. Since there is no one "best way" to teach reading (or anything else for that matter), tailor these techniques to your curriculum, your students, and your teaching style.

Sharon Faber

Helping Struggling Readers

For many teachers, teaching strategies are intuitive and based simply on the need to cope with day-to-day challenges in the classroom. *(The "strategy" evolves as the day evolves.)* Therefore, if a student cannot read, the teacher develops a strategy to deal with the situation. The teacher might *"cover"* by making the textbook or content come alive for the entire class, so that the non-readers' lack of reading skill is irrelevant. Teachers make sure that students learn the important basic content, but are rarely able (or trained) to address the fundamental issue at hand:

If students cannot read, they cannot learn independently.

Many teachers use reading strategies without realizing what they are doing. Every time a teacher breaks down a textbook into manageable units, highlights the features of a textbook, or provides specific content-related vocabulary from a textbook, that teacher is introducing valuable reading strategies.

Of course teachers recognize that most students who cannot read are very smart in many other ways. They can recite every word verbatim from their favorite movies or CDs and are quite surprisingly skilled at imitating their teachers' facial expressions, voices, and mannerisms. The students are not lacking in intelligence, so teachers assign projects, group work, graphic organizers, tapes, videos, or anything they can think of to help the students learn using modalities other than reading.

In this way, many well-meaning teachers unknowingly set their struggling readers up for future failure by doing two things:

- Not dealing with the problems for students in their own classroom

- Allowing students with reading disabilities to move forward to the next teacher *(who may not care if they cannot read)*

Today, everyone is so concerned about state and national standards, standardized tests, and how students score, that teachers, pressured and preoccupied with students reaching standards and showing improvement, often forget that students who do not score well **may be under-performing because they cannot read the questions on the test—not because they were not familiar with the material.**

All teachers—in **all** content areas—must adopt the attitude that any child who comes into their class with a reading disability is their responsibility. Teachers must show students how to use thinking and reading strategies that will enable them to comprehend the content as well as the individual words. They must model the thinking processes they use when reading for content so students can learn by example. Teachers must encourage students to think about how great writers, historians, scientists, and mathematicians process information and arrive at conclusions.

If you are worried that this practice will inhibit individual student creativity, I say, "SO WHAT?" Don't you remember what it was like in student teaching when were were forced to do those extensive lesson plans? We knew that "real teachers" wrote notes in a little box in a plan book, but we had to write full lesson plans so we could learn every step of the process. This process forced us to think carefully about every step in the teaching process and choose specific strategies that would work best for each different type of content or lesson. In teaching reading to middle school students, as well as teaching student teachers, creativity comes only after mastering the fundamentals. Learning to read is a process, and content is the vehicle teachers use to drive that process toward creativity and comprehension.

Good teachers have been teaching reading strategies in their content areas for many years without realizing what they were doing. Good teachers have always shown their students the way textbooks are put together in their subjects, and how to use the features in their texts. They give their students specific vocabulary critical to the content; they focus on the major concepts needed to understand specific subjects. Every time these good teachers use one of these instructional activities, they are teaching their students to use reading strategies.

In How to Teach Reading When You're Not a Reading Teacher, *my goal is to make middle grades teachers aware of which reading strategies they already use, then introduce additional strategies they can incorporate into any subject area. Using current research on teaching reading and how students learn, the practical approach presented here is focused primarily on teaching reading to 10- through 14-year-olds. Middle grades teachers know that in order to teach middle grades students they must understand their physical, intellectual, emotional, and social development. But, before we get to specific reading research, I'd like to make a few observations about middle school kids.*

DID YOU KNOW?

Researcher Benjamin Bloom says that 13 is the most critical age for students because of hormones, peer pressures, and social forces.

My Experience with Middle School Readers

After I had been teaching a few years, I began to be able to identify my students' reading ability as early as the first day of school, and I could do this without their ever having to open a book! Based on my experience, I have developed a theory that I think may be true on the first day of school for all middle school teachers. I call it "The Three Reading Groups Theory."

My "scientific method" (remember, I am an English teacher) was to hypothesize that my students generally fell into three groups. I based these groups on where the students chose to sit on the first day of school before I made my seating chart. Think about your classes and see if this description fits your students.

Kids Who Choose the Desks in the Front of the Room

The kids who choose to sit in the front of the room come from homes where parents value education and school success. These are the kids who have been read to, whose homes are stocked with magazines, books, and newspapers, and who have been on vacations with their families. Their parents have taught them the rules of school, such as:

- *Sit up front.*
- *Laugh at the teacher's jokes.*
- *Do your homework.*
- *Don't make crude noises in public.*
- *Act like you like the teacher.*
- *Raise your hand before you answer a question.*

These kids come to school and know that it is important! In fact, these are the kids who always say things like, "I love school; I love to learn; you are my favorite teacher."

In teacher terms, these students are "reading ready," and I call them **Red Birds**. *(By the way, most teachers fit in this category when they take graduate courses.)*

Kids Who Choose the Desks in the Middle of the Room

The kids who choose to sit in the middle of the room are almost as delightful as the Red Birds up front. The only real difference I have found with the kids in the middle is that they also choose to do only as much work or to behave only as well as will keep teachers off their cases.

These kids tend to be realists who know they have to go to school because that's what kids do, it's the law. They come every day to see their friends, they do the required work at a minimal level, and they behave right to the limits of their teachers' tolerance levels.

Most students are in this middle group, and in teacher terms, they are "almost reading ready." I call this middle group the **Blue Birds**.

Kids Who Choose the Desks in the Back of the Room

As we all know, the farther back you go in your class (or in a faculty meeting), the more at-risk the kids (teachers) become. The kids who choose these seats want to be invisible. They wear coats and hoods on their heads in 100-degree heat. They wish they could disappear into the back wall and they don't want you to mess with them.

Many of these kids have attitude problems. Their body language often says it all! Their heads are on their desks, or they are slouched over their desks with their legs stretched out. Their faces reflect their boredom. By the time they have reached middle school, for many of these kids, it isn't "I cannot read," it has become "I will not read."

These kids have to save face at all costs. No wonder some of them have become discipline problems. School has not been a good place for them to be, and for any number of reasons (many of them out of our control), they have decided that they will just stay in school until they are old enough to drop out.

In teacher terms, they are "not reading ready." They are at a high risk of failure and are probably struggling, or non-readers. I call these unfortunate kids in the back of the room **Could Become Jailbirds***. Our prisons are full of people who dropped out of school. Sadly, some of these kids have the potential to become one of those statistics.*

Year after year, I saw these same three reading groups in my classes. I did everything I could to make my class a successful experience for all of them. As I worked closely with these kids, I realized that at different times, there were struggling readers in all three groups. My students' ability to read depended on the text they were reading. Even my good readers struggled when they read difficult or unknown text. (I still remember how I hated my statistics book in college and how hard I struggled to make sense out of all that gibberish!) I found that many of my students—although they could already read at varying levels—also needed to be taught specifically what they were doing as they read successfully, so they could help themselves later when the text became more difficult.

There are many explanations for why some kids cannot read by the time they are in middle school. However, one of the reasons is often that when they were taught to read in elementary school, they were not ready to learn the skills. Just like their teachers, students are all very different. They come in all shapes and sizes and, especially in the case of middle graders, at a difficult time in their lives.

Middle school teachers must take them where they are developmentally (physically, intellectually, emotionally, and socially) and help them become the best learners they can be. **It is important to teach reading strategies intentionally.**

If teachers truly believe that they make a difference—*and I do*—then teaching students reading skills and strategies must become an important part of instruction in every subject. *This book is my way of sharing ideas that I have collected on how middle school teachers can accomplish this awesome task.*

"Setting a goal is not the main thing.
It is deciding how you will go about
achieving it and staying with that plan
that spells success."

— *Tom Landry, football coach*

CHAPTER 1

THE RESEARCH

"To begin with the end in mind means to start with a
clear understanding of your destination. It means to
know where you're going so that you better
understand where you are now so that the steps you
take are always in the right direction."

— *Stephen Covey*

What Is Your Reading I.Q.?

Here are ten simple statements about reading. Based on prior knowledge about reading comprehension, decide whether each statement is true or false. This is a pre-assessment, so mark each question even if you are not certain of the answer. By the time you finish this book, you will know the correct answers. Some of them may even surprise you.

Reading Quiz

T or F 1. Content reading strategies are useful only with printed text.

T or F 2. If students have not developed a strong inner voice, they will mumble and move their lips as they read.

T or F 3. Many students have difficulty reading aloud and comprehending at the same time.

T or F 4. Prior knowledge is an important part of reading comprehension.

T or F 5. When good readers read, they look at every letter and every word.

T or F 6. Readers must know what most of the words mean before they can understand what they are reading.

T or F 7. Comprehension is selective. Good readers focus on important information, and poor readers focus only on their interest in the text.

T or F 8. Good readers examine the structure of words and use roots and affixes to help comprehend new words.

T or F 9. Reading strategies and skills should be taught explicitly and systematically to both good and poor readers.

T or F 10. Only trained reading teachers, working in pull-out program, can teach struggling readers to read at the middle and high school levels, because it's too late to teach them them to read in their content classes.

Understanding the Research

"That the brain learns to read at all attests to its remarkable ability to sift through seemingly confusing input and establish patterns and systems. For a few children, this process comes naturally; most have to be taught."

— *David Sousa*

Learning to read text is both a difficult and unnatural process for the brain. According to the National Institute for Literacy and the Center for Education Statistics, over 40 million adults in the United States are functionally illiterate, and approximately 40 percent of fourth graders lack the most basic reading skills. Walberg and Tsai identified a phenomenon in education that is called the "Matthew Effect" (Walberg and Tsai, 1983), which is based on the line from the Bible that says that "the rich get richer and the poor get poorer." It means that the gap between children who are good readers and those who are poor readers gets wider and wider as they move through school. Those who cannot read fall farther and farther behind their peers and are then less and less motivated to become good readers. In fact, high school graduation rates can be predicted with reasonable accuracy by assessing a child's reading skill at the end of third grade. If a child is not reading on grade level by the fourth grade, he is quite unlikely to graduate from high school.

 DID YOU KNOW?

If students are identified as low-achieving by the third grade, they remain in that group throughout their schooling unless a future teacher recognizes their potential.

The National Reading Panel (2000) defined reading comprehension as "intentional thinking during which meaning is constructed through interaction between the text and the reader." The panel also explained that "the content of meaning is influenced by the text and by the reader's prior knowledge and experience that are brought to bear on it" and that "reading is purposeful and active." In other words, readers derive meaning from text when they engage in intentional, problem-solving thinking processes. Reading comprehension can be improved by instruction in using specific cognitive strategies or in using reasoning strategies when encountering barriers to understanding. To ensure that all children can read, there must be focused instruction from knowledgeable and skilled teachers at all grade levels.

Comprehension has two levels:

- Literal Comprehension
    Identifying individual words and their meanings, as determined by immediate context

- Higher-order Comprehension
    When analytic, evaluative, and reflective comprehension occurs

The skills necessary to achieve literal comprehension are just as important as those necessary for the higher-order comprehension processes. For children to become good readers, they must develop a number of skills that work together during the reading process. Children should be taught reading in developmentally appropriate ways. This instruction should be aimed at the students' zone of proximal development, a level identified by Vygotsky(1978) just above where the student works successfully independently.

An excellent and painless place to learn about reading research is in the 2001 report, *Put Reading First: The Research Building Blocks for Teaching Children to Read*. Published as a guide for teachers, it is reader-friendly and describes the findings of the *National Reading Panel Report (2000), Teaching Children to Read*. It summarizes the findings from scientifically-based research on how to successfully teach children to read. *Put Reading First* provides analysis and discussion in five areas of reading instruction: phonemic awareness, phonics, fluency, vocabulary, and text comprehension. It defines each skill is defined, reviews the evidence from the research, and gives implications for classroom instruction along with descriptions of proven strategies for teaching each skill.

Don't be misled by the cover, which says *Kindergarten through Grade Three*. This easy-to-read explanation of reading is exactly what teachers of any content, at any grade level need if they have struggling readers. It is a must-read for anyone who wants to learn about reading instruction, and it is simple enough that even if teachers have never had a reading course, they will be able to understand it! Go online and get a free copy at www.nifl.gov.

> *I have found that whenever you read books on how to teach reading, the authors consistently identify five essential components of effective reading instruction. These components, the same five identified by Put Reading First, are based on scientific research, and in order for kids to learn to read well, explicit and systematic instruction must be provided in all five areas. Since I was trained as a secondary teacher, when I began learning about how to work with my struggling readers, the only areas of reading instruction I recognized by name in the five were vocabulary development and comprehension. My guess is that many of you are in the same boat I was in—secondary-trained content people, so it is critical that we understand what learning to read is all about if we are going to help our students.*

The following sections provide a brief overview of the five essential components of effective reading instruction.

Area 1: Phonemic Awareness

For most content area teachers *(as opposed to a trained reading teacher or an elementary teacher)*, phonemic awareness may be a new concept. What is **phonemic awareness**? All these big words mean is that in order to be able to read, kids must be able to hear the sounds that letters make when they are put together to make words. When letter sounds are written in books, they look like this: /b/. The marks on each side mean that you say the sound, not the letter name, so the word "bat" would be written /b/a/t/ if you wanted to show that you should say the word **phonemically**, or using the letter sounds. This is the kind of thing that kindergarten and first grade teachers do with students all the time when they teach them to blend and substitute sounds to make words. The sounds of the letters are called **phonemes**.

Students need to know that all spoken words consist of these phonemes, or individual sounds. They need to hear how words can be **segmented** (pulled apart) into sounds, and how these sounds can be **blended** (put back together) and **manipulated** (added, deleted, and substituted) to create and read a variety of words. Students need to know how to blend sounds to read words and to segment sounds in words to spell them.

Area 2: Phonics

The second important element for reading is *phonics*. Phonics is the relationship between the sounds heard when spoken (**phonemes**) and the letters in the alphabet (**graphemes**). Phonics instruction follows phonemic awareness. Children who cannot hear and work with the phonemes of spoken words will have a difficult time learning how to relate these phonemes to the graphemes when they see them in written form. Children who are able to understand how sounds and letters work together to make words can usually recognize familiar words and are often better able to decode unfamiliar words.

While most teachers have heard the term **phonics** and have a general idea of what phonics is, at the middle school level teachers usually do not teach phonics to students except to occasionally help them sound out a new word. It is likely that teachers who help students sound out words do this because they were taught that way in school—not because they have studied how to teach phonics. If that is true, it is also likely that teachers who were not taught to sound out words when they learned to read, probably do not suggest their students do it.

> *The more I've learned about good readers, the more convinced I've become that phonemic awareness and phonics are critical, and we must incorporate teaching these strategies into our own content areas.*

Area 3: Vocabulary Development

Vocabulary development involves teaching kids to store information about the meanings and pronunciation of words necessary to understand a given content. Many teachers think that vocabulary development means giving students words only in the content area that they need to know, having them look up the definitions in the dictionary, writing their own sentences using the words, and/or having them find the words in sentences in the textbook or whatever text they are reading. Some teachers even go so far as to teach students the difference in the **denotation** (dictionary definition) and **connotation** (real-life usage) of the words. Once the process of teaching reading becomes clear, it is obvious that just having students do these things does not really mean that they will **learn** the words. Instead, the result is a group of students who can pass a weekly test, but two weeks *(or two hours)* later, they will not recognize many of the words or retain the words' meanings.

Area 4: Fluency (Including Oral Reading Skills)

Fluency means that students can read text with accuracy, expression, speed, and with comprehension. Fluency also means that when students are reading aloud they can read with the proper **inflection**: group words into meaningful phrases, observe punctuation, and read with expression so that the listener can enjoy the reading. Their reading sounds natural, as if they were speaking. Fluency changes depending on what material readers are reading and their familiarity with the words and text. Even skilled readers may not be able to read some texts, like legal or technical material, fluently.

Fluency is important because it provides a bridge between recognizing words and comprehension. Fluent readers do not have to concentrate on decoding words, so they can focus their attention on the content. They make connections between the ideas in the text and their own personal experience and knowledge as they read. Less fluent readers must focus longer on figuring out the words, leaving little time, attention, or energy to comprehend the text.

At the middle grades level, some students can say the words when they read them, but their reading aloud is a painful experience for those listening because they lack fluency. They read slowly, word by word, and their oral reading is choppy and plodding.

Area 5: Reading Comprehension Strategies

Reading comprehension strategies are sets of steps that good readers use to make sense of what they are reading. These strategies help good readers understand, remember, and explain to others what they have read. The only problem with comprehension strategies is that good readers tend to use them without really thinking about what they are doing. These strategies can be taught to students, but teachers must know the steps to teach them. Classroom teachers must learn what the effective reading strategies are, what steps are involved in each strategy, and how to model the steps so that students can use them when they read.

Reading strategies need to be flexible and adaptable to meet the needs of any reading problem regardless of the content. Many factors like topic familiarity (prior knowledge), text and picture support, number of unfamiliar words, and teacher support are also important to reading comprehension. Remember that good readers use a variety of strategies when they read. It is the teacher's responsibility to help students learn which strategies work particularly well for each type of content.

> "Many excellent third-grade readers will falter or fail in later grade academic tasks if the teaching of reading is neglected in the middle and secondary grades."
>
> — *Reading Next, page 3*

> "Very few older struggling readers need help to read the words on a page; their most common problem is that they are not able to comprehend what they read."
>
> — *Reading Next, page 3*

Summarizing Reading to Learn Research

Another important document for all secondary teachers to read is the 2004 Carnegie Corporation report, *Reading Next: A Vision for Action and Research in Middle and High School Literacy*. According to the report, secondary educators must figure out how to teach students how to:

- read with a purpose, select materials of interest and learn from those materials, figure out the meanings of new words,
- differentiate fact from opinion, resolve conflicting content in different texts, and
- integrate the new information they are learning with information they already know.

Teachers must help students make the shift from the early grades' focus of *"learning to read"* to the next step of *"reading to learn."* The goal for secondary teachers is to teach students how to comprehend the specific subject area content in their classes. The *Reading Next* authors emphasize that the real challenge in helping older students read to learn is based on two distinct differences in young children and the pre-adolescents and adolescents:

- First, older students implement literacy skills that are more complex and comprehend content that is more embedded than elementary text.
- Second, older students are not as motivated to read or as interested in reading school text.

Simply put, the content textbooks in our classes are not as easy to read or as interesting as the books and stories students got to read in elementary school.

The *Reading Next* report not only reviews the current research and practice in the field of literacy, but it focuses on elements aimed at improving middle and high school literacy achievement. The authors stress that there is not one best combination of the elements. No one knows even how many of the elements must be present for readers to be successful. Teachers must try out various combinations of the elements to see which combination works best for their students. The elements are divided into two categories: instructional improvements and infrastructure improvements (*Reading Next*, page 12).

Improving Reading Instruction

Instructional Improvements	Infrastructure Improvements
• Direct, explicit comprehension instruction	• Extended time for literacy
• Effective instructional principles embedded in content	• Professional development
• Motivation and self-directed reading	• Ongoing summative assessment of students and programs
• Text-based collaborative learning	• Teacher teams
• Strategic tutoring	• Leadership
• Diverse texts	• Comprehensive and coordinated literacy programs
• Intensive writing	
• Technology components	
• Ongoing formative assessment	

Although the report outlines fifteen elements, it makes clear that three of the elements are important building blocks and without these three, there will be no success in implementing a middle or high school literacy program (*Reading Next*, page 29).

1. **Professional development—**
   "Without appropriate and ongoing professional development, instructional innovations are unlikely to be sustained or even initially implemented effectively."

2. **Ongoing formative assessment of students—**
   ". . . if instruction is not closely informed by ongoing formative assessment, it is too likely that teachers will overlook important gaps and improvements in students' skills and knowledge, undermining the efficacy of instructional innovations."

3. **Ongoing summative assessment of students and programs—**
   ". . . ongoing summative assessment is required for accountability purposes in order to evaluate the effectiveness of programs overall, for subgroups of students, and for individual students."

If you want a copy of *Reading Next*, it can be downloaded at *www.all4ed.org*.

Why should you know the research when all you need is a quick fix for your classroom? Ask yourself, would you go to a tax accountant who hadn't kept up with the latest tax laws? Would you go to a surgeon who hadn't kept up with the latest surgical techniques? The answer is probably a resounding NO. You don't want to be one of the teachers who has used the same materials and strategies for years! Teachers cannot expect parents to trust them to do the best job of educating their children if they haven't kept up with the latest on "what works" in their fields.

Translating the Research into Practice

The implications of research provide clearcut guidelines for effective teaching at the middle school level. First, our brains remember what is used frequently, and students develop procedural knowledge through repeated practice or rehearsals. As students practice recalling facts or procedures, the material becomes part of their long-term memory and, therefore, automatic. While some "drill" is important, students who employ strategies to recall information tend to remember what they have learned. Teachers must provide a wide range of activities and offer various strategy options for students. These options will allow them to

- become familiar with forms and uses of written language,

- develop language and metacognition skills required for comprehension, to learn how words are structured and represented in print,

- become enthusiastic about learning to read and write, and

- apply reading strategies in new situations or when learning becomes difficult.

Secondly, at the middle grades level, content area teachers find many students who have trouble expressing themselves effectively after reading. Many students cannot think critically about the content and therefore, are unable to either make inferences from their reading or process the complex material. For these students, teachers must begin with basic reading strategies. The students must practice the reading strategies, repeating them until they become automatic. A primary goal for all teachers should be to make sure that all students know the appropriate reading strategies for each type of content.

Research says that for students to become good readers, they need to learn strategies that will teach them how to:

- read narrative and expository text,

- understand and retain what they read,

- connect their own knowledge and experience to the text,

- use the strategies flexibly and in combination,

- be persistent in trying different strategies until they find one that works, and

- communicate with others about what they read.

During the past ten years, research by neuroscientists has expanded what we know about those areas in relation to the human brain. Scientists have studied which brain areas are most active during which types of educational tasks (Sousa, 1999). Specialists have identified brain regions that are associated with such learning activities as language, reading, math, motor learning, music appreciation, or verbal responses to questions in a classroom discussion (Sousa, 2001). This extensive research has provided educators with some consistent answers about which instructional strategies work best.

In their book, *Classroom Instruction That Works: Research-Based Strategies for Increasing Student Achievement,* (ASCD, 2001) Marzano, Pickering, and Pollack identified nine categories of instructional strategies that were proven to improve student achievement:

1. Identifying similarities and differences

2. Summarizing and note taking

3. Reinforcing effort and providing recognition

4. Completing homework

5. Representing knowledge

6. Participating in learning groups

7. Setting objectives and
   providing feedback

8. Generating and testing hypotheses

9. Using cues, questions, and
   advance organizers

Variations of these nine instructional strategies are found throughout the research on reading, and a number of these instructional practices are rooted in brain-compatible research (Sousa, 1999). However, it is critical to note one additional research finding. Research shows that students must be involved with their own learning and take personal responsibility for their achievement, so teachers must assure that students can use the reading strategies at an independent level. Then students can choose which strategy works best for them in each specific situation.

"Patience is a necessary
ingredient of genius."

— *Benjamin Disraeli*

CHAPTER 2

CONTENT AREA READING

"You can read to a child and he is entertained for a while,
but if you teach a child to read, he can learn for a lifetime."

— *Conrad Faber*

What Is Content Area Reading?

How is content area reading different from any reading? Content area reading requires helping students make connections between what they already know and the new information being presented. Content teachers need to teach their students how to use reading as a tool for thinking and learning in their specific subjects. Content area teachers must help students read their textbooks and additional materials effectively in order to understand the content. That means that teachers must do much more than just assign pages to read, lecture, and ask questions to see if students have read the assignment. More importantly, teachers must help students link reading and new learning to other content areas.

To get good at something, one must do that thing often and practice doing it well. Thus, to become a good reader, a student must read. Reading is an interaction that happens among the reader, the text, and the content. When they read a great deal, students become good readers. Unfortunately, at the middle grades level, many students read only when their teachers make them read. If they do not practice, students will have trouble reading in content area classes for a variety of reasons. They have trouble understanding the author's ideas, and since they have not had much experience with the topic, they cannot make connections with their personal lives and create meaning for new ideas. In addition, struggling readers prejudge the reading materials as too hard or too boring.

Three Factors That Affect Content Area Learning

At the middle grades level, all teachers deal with content area literacy. **Content area literacy** is the level of reading and writing necessary for students to read and comprehend the instructional materials used in content areas. Content area literacy engages students in learning new knowledge. Through the elementary schools, most students learned how to read. In middle school they must use their reading skills to learn the content of their subjects. Three factors affect this content area learning: the teacher, the student, and the content.

Factor One: The Teacher

As in all learning, the teacher is an important factor. In the middle grades classroom, the teacher must have a sound understanding of:

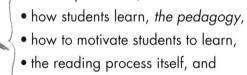

- the subject matter,
- how students learn, *the pedagogy,*
- how to motivate students to learn,
- the reading process itself, and
- the specific developmental characteristics of the students they teach.
  (When it is understood that most of the things that middle grades students do to drive teachers crazy are perfectly normal behaviors for this age group, teachers can better understand how to teach them.)

Teachers must take an active role in both the teaching and the learning process. They must motivate, instruct, and guide their students in their classes. They must help students learn to monitor what makes sense as they read, how the new information connects with what they already know, and what techniques work for them. Middle grades teachers must provide strategies to help students organize and systematize new learning. Teachers who do this will help students become active learners able to access accurate, lasting, and useful knowledge.

Teaching reading is complex. It requires a good knowledge of research and how to apply that research. It takes time and hard work to practice effective reading strategies. To teach reading effectively, middle grades teachers must connect what needs to be learned with the students' lives and interests. This means teachers must know their students and the cultures in which they live. All students come to the classroom with different backgrounds, and they construct their own understanding of what they are learning based on their prior social and academic experiences. They bring with them what they have learned outside the classroom and what they have already learned in school. It is the role of the teacher to help students understand the process they move through as they internalize information to explain, clarify, or make predictions about what they are learning.

The goal is to get students to think as they read. This requires that teachers get students actively engaged in the learning process. One way to do this is to get them interested and excited about what they are learning. This interest and excitement will happen if teachers are passionate and enthusiastic about what they teach and, then, pass that enthusiasm on to their students.

Factor Two: The Student

The second factor that impacts content area learning is the student *(and what each one brings to the classroom)*. The student's prior knowledge and experiences, language development, reading ability, and attitudes toward school are all critical elements in content area learning.

As any middle grades teacher knows, working with students is a challenge: middle grades kids have unique physical, intellectual, emotional, and social characteristics and issues. Knowing the characteristics of this age group is imperative for middle grades teachers. While it is tempting for middle grades teachers to say they know their students "because they work with them day after day," how many teachers have actually studied the characteristics of these students?

Content area teachers must understand the middle grades students they are teaching so that they know which reading skills are best for **their** students to understand **their** material. They need to help students by teaching appropriate study skills and effective strategies for reading, writing, organizing, and test taking. Readers construct meaning as they read.

Teachers must provide support for individual students, or both the teacher and the students will become frustrated and feel like they have failed. Good readers predict, organize information, and interact with the text. They evaluate what they are reading **based on what they already know**. They change how they read, **based on their interests** and whether they are having any problems understanding the reading. So the bottom line to teaching content area reading is first knowing to whom you are teaching it.

Factor Three: The Content

The third factor which affects content reading is the content. The content is presented in the text and materials used in classes. The text's quality, clarity, writing style, scope and sequence, content, format, organization, and patterns are critical (Barton and Billmeyer, 1998). These materials used as the vehicles for the content are very important and need to be selected and taught with care.

In today's educational setting, it is important to note that while many middle grades students seem to retain content and perform well on teachers' tests during the year, their standardized test scores do not reflect what teachers thought the students had learned. The content itself must be complete, interesting, and meaningful so that it transfers to new situations—so that students can apply content understanding, not just regurgitate facts.

DID YOU KNOW?

Learning is cemented after 17 to 41 rehearsals.

How Is Content Area Reading Taught?

Once students reach the intermediate grades, they meet approximately 10,000 new words, words never before encountered in print, in school reading each year. Most of these words are big words, words of seven or more letters and two or more syllables.

—Cunningham

When thinking about content area reading with the middle grades teacher, the middle grades student, and middle grades content in mind, it becomes very clear that teachers in every subject must help students by supporting them before, during, and after their reading experiences. Before assigning reading, teachers need to read the content themselves from a middle grades student's perspective. Every teacher needs to take a routine, fresh look at the reading. *Pretend that the material is written in a foreign language. For many students content reading looks like it's written in a foreign language.*

The challenge is to figure out how to help students understand the content. Teachers should look at the content through the students' eyes, not from their own personal perspective after studying the same subject for years. That simple refocusing will help teachers better determine which strategies students will need to construct meaning.

Three Important Elements for Content Area Reading

Just like learning, reading is an active process because comprehension requires more than just saying the words on a page. Effective readers
- interact with the text while they read it,
- work to make sense of what they are reading, and
- apply reading strategies to help them understand the information when the reading gets too difficult.

Every content area teacher must carefully consider and plan for three elements when teaching lessons involving any kind of reading: prior knowledge, classroom learning environment, and text features.

Considering Prior Knowledge

Prior knowledge is the content knowledge and personal experience that a reader brings to the text. When students read new information, they make sense of it by seeing how it connects with what they already know. Students do not bring the same backgrounds or experiences to school, so no two of them will comprehend anything they read the same way. Reading for meaning is not simply moving eyes over the words on a page. Deriving meaning requires making connections.

> *Have you read those same ideas before? They are so important that they bear repeating several times!*

The more prior knowledge a reader brings to the classroom, the more he learns and remembers from what he reads. Since a lack of experience can become a barrier to learning new concepts or ideas, teachers need to find creative ways to help students develop and expand their knowledge base through direct exposure to discussions, analogies, and original explanations of content area concepts. Content area teachers need to provide students a variety of opportunities to work with and experience concepts in context and to explore the relationships between them.

The first step is to prepare students for reading by incorporating pre-reading strategies that activate and assess the learners' prior knowledge. This way, students can have a structure on which to attach new learning. Common pre-reading strategies used by content area teachers are:

- brainstorming
- asking questions
- providing analogies
- discussing the topic as a class

How to Teach Reading . . .

These pre-reading strategies benefit all students because those who have limited prior knowledge can learn from their more experienced peers. Students can even teach each other as they use the strategies.

Using pre-reading strategies also helps teachers discover any misconceptions or inaccurate information students may have about a certain topic. As teachers use pre-reading strategies, students and teachers learn which strategies work well for them and for the content area and practice them.

Good readers know that they must think about what they are reading before, during, and after they read it. Many middle grades students are not aware of this need. Teachers must teach students how to monitor their own understanding at all three stages. When students monitor their own understanding, they can consciously adapt and modify their reading according to what and why they are reading. Struggling readers have to be taught not only how to monitor their understanding, but also which strategies will help them increase understanding while they read.

Considering the Classroom Learning Environment

Middle grades students must feel safe physically, intellectually, emotionally, and socially if they are going to learn in their classes. All students learn best when they feel accepted by their teachers and peers in an atmosphere where making mistakes and thinking in different ways is acceptable. Middle grades teachers must create a sense of safety, acceptance, and order for their students.

Research has identified specific classroom attributes that create a positive learning environment. The following chart lists the attributes and their implications for teachers.

Creating a Positive Learning Environment

Students need to have:	Implications for the Teacher:
Precise academic expectations and instructions	Explain what students will be doing with the information they read in the text (i.e., for a test, to write a paper, to give an oral presentation, or to present a project, and so on). Provide necessary background knowledge prior to the reading if they do not have it.
A purpose for the assignments	Explain why students are reading (i.e., to learn facts, to make a comparison, to look for the theme, for enjoyment, etc.). This will help to determine which reading strategies to use, the pace of reading, the type of mental questions to ask and answer while reading, and how to monitor for understanding.
Relevant assignments	Explain what students will gain from learning the content (thereby increasing their motivation and interest). Provide the opportunity for students to read text for real reasons.
A consistent routine	Show students how to chunk work into manageable pieces and how to figure out what new words mean. Teach them to follow a step-by-step process for analyzing and processing what they are reading.
Confidence in their ability to complete tasks successfully	Students learn best what is personally meaningful to them in a positive emotional climate.
Clearly articulated classroom rules	Content area classrooms should become supportive environments for comprehension development.
A chance to learn and interact together	New learning occurs best when students have the opportunity to interact and share with each other. When students verbalize their ideas, it allows them to deepen their understanding and it also provides students with an opportunity to compare their thinking with the teacher and with one another.

Considering Text Features

Text features differ from subject to subject, so the reading skills and strategies students use will also change from subject to subject. Sentence structure and vocabulary are different. Science and social studies texts are often above the reading level of many students. While math books may have grade-specific math concepts, the reading level can be above that of the students as well. Again, when planning lessons, teachers need to look at their content as if they were the students, rather than the experts. They need to consider which reading skills the students will need to understand what they are reading. Content area teachers must analyze the text features of the books before assigning reading.

Authors often organize their text by patterns. Common patterns found in textbooks are:

- comparison/contrast
- descriptive pattern
- episode pattern
- time sequence
- process/cause-effect
- general to specific

Knowing which pattern is being used helps the reader to locate information, separate important and unimportant information, sequence events in a logical order, and link new information to what is already known. Content area teachers need to teach students the difference in narrative and informational text, typical patterns used in the textbooks, how to recognize the different organizational patterns, and the kinds of questions that each pattern is intended to help answer.

The Question of Vocabulary

One of the most important aspects of text features is vocabulary. All content area teachers need to focus on vocabulary instruction. Each content has its own unique vocabulary, terminology, and language, particularly the labels used to identify important content area concepts. If students understand the content-specific vocabulary before they read, comprehension improves. Very often, content vocabulary consists of major concepts that set up a lesson or unit. Students must have a clear understanding of what these concepts mean. Also, content area vocabulary terms often need focused attention because they are rarely part of the content that students already know. Sometimes, content area terms are semantically related: if one science or math term is understood, others can be connected and understood.

Many teachers have students look up words in glossaries or dictionaries, but actually this is the least effective way to help students transfer the new words into their everyday language. Looking up a word does not aid understanding or long-term recall because it separates the learning of vocabulary from the subject matter. Just defining words is not enough to understand concepts. Students need strategies that can help them learn what new concepts mean and see the connections between these concepts.

Four levels of word recognition for students were identified by Dale & O'Rourke (1986) and Nagy (1988):

Four Levels of Word Recognition

Level Four Full Word Knowledge	Students understand the meaning of the word and how it changes in different contexts.
Level Three Partial Word Knowledge	Students know the word in context and can use it in their writing.
Level Two Initial Recognition	Students recognize the word and may be able to pronounce it, but they do not know its meaning.
Level One Unknown Word	Students cannot read or recognize the word.

Students develop knowledge about a word gradually as they have repeated exposure to it. They move from not knowing the word at all to recognizing that they have seen the word before. Once the word is somewhat familiar, they develop partial knowledge, in which they have a general sense of what the word means, or they know at least one meaning. When students have full word knowledge, they know multiple meanings and can use the word in a variety of ways.

Teachers can help students learn new content-specific vocabulary directly through explicit instruction. They can teach vocabulary at the beginning of a unit of study, during the lesson, or after the text has been read. Regardless of the timing of the vocabulary instruction, students learn content area terms best through purposeful interaction with these concepts through field trips, guest speakers, or, visuals such as video, movies, or Internet research (Brozo and Simpson, 2003).

After vocabulary terms are selected, teachers need to choose strategies that will help students learn the concepts and their relationships to each other. Nagy, Anderson, and Herman (1987) identified six types of context clues that teachers should teach their students to use:

- Definition
- Logic
- Example/illustration
- Root words and affixes
- Contrast
- Grammar

No matter which vocabulary strategies content area teachers use, they need to make word study active. Students not only need to expand their knowledge of words, but they also need to understand words well enough to be able to use them appropriately during their everyday lives.

Teachers should limit the number of words taught at one time *(quality not quantity)* and concentrate on key concepts. The concepts need to be taught in semantically-related clusters so students can see related concepts. Teachers need to model how to determine a word's meaning in text material by thinking aloud and sharing the thinking process they use to understand the word with their students. Teach students not only how to use glossaries and dictionaries appropriately, but also how to use those sources to figure out what new words mean.

CHAPTER 2

Playing the Blame Game

In 1989, Irvin and Connors reported that, "Although it is unreasonable to expect that any student could acquire enough reading competence by the fifth grade to carry him or her through middle school, high school, and adult life, almost half of the middle schools offer no systematic reading instruction or make it available only for remedial readers or as an elective."

This statement was made in 1989, but, unfortunately, it seems that it still holds true today. In far too many middle schools, there are teachers who continue to believe that teaching reading is "not their job."

> *We have all heard colleagues say things like, "But I can't do everything! How can I be expected to teach these kids the curriculum and get them ready for state tests if I have to teach them to read at the same time? They should already know how to read when I get them! If their parents and the elementary schools had done what they were supposed to do, I wouldn't have these problems." For those of you who have heard these things said, let's talk about the blame game.*

When students arrive in kindergarten and first grade and are not "reading ready," some elementary teachers blame the parents. *(The parents may not have the knowledge or skills themselves to be able to help their children get ready to read.)* Many of the parents complain about teachers "not doing what they're supposed to be doing." From the time these children are in kindergarten through fifth grade, teachers work hard to overcome the deficiencies *(most of them out of teacher control)* with which many of their students started school. And sometimes, no matter how hard these elementary teachers work, a few students pass through to middle grades without being able to read at the appropriate grade level.

When these kids get to the middle grades, some middle grades teachers blame the elementary schools. The middle grades teachers work hard to overcome the deficiencies *(again, most of them out of teacher control)* with which many students graduated from elementary school. No matter how hard they try, a few students pass to high school as poor or struggling readers. Then, of course, when they get to high school, the high school teachers

How to Teach Reading . . .

blame the middle grades teachers. Then, the high school teachers do their best to overcome the deficiencies with which the students arrive at high school. And, again, no matter what they try, a few students go on to college and have to take pre-college English, writing, and math classes before they can take college classes. It is a never-ending cycle of blame that can be stopped if all content area teachers realize that regardless of their grade level and what happened before, struggling or non-readers are their responsibility.

Great athletes *(like Michael Jordan, Tiger Woods, and Wayne Gretzky)* begin by learning the basics in their sports *(like dribbling, putting, and passing the puck)*. These athletes practice the basic moves until they become automatic habits. Once the basics become second nature, the athletes are able to expand their skills and become superstars on the basketball court, golf course, and hockey rink.

In this same manner, middle grades teachers should think of their students as "athletes" at the beginning of their careers in reading. In teaching reading, teachers must take students through the same process that the athletes experience. By practicing basic content reading strategies until they become automatic, students will gain the skills they need to become superstars in any subject *(even when they take standardized tests)*.

Harry Wong says, "The number one problem in the classroom is not discipline, it is the lack of procedures and routines." A similar thing may be said about reading:

The number one problem with students is not their inability to read, it is their lack of basic reading strategies.

The primary goal of all teachers is to make sure that their students are taught reading strategies and are able to use the appropriate reading strategies in each content area.

CHARACTERISTICS OF A GOOD READER

"One who fears failure limits his worth.
Failure is the opportunity
to begin again more intelligently."

— *Henry Ford*

What Makes a Good Reader?

Good readers are engaged actively in what they are reading. <u>Their minds have a movie playing as they read</u>: they hear the characters' voices, see the setting, and participate in the events.

exactly *This is why so many readers are disappointed when they see a movie or documentary of a book or something they studied or read: the scenery or actors do not look or sound like the people they had pictured in their minds when they read.*

Good readers in social studies and science can watch documentaries or scientific shows on Discovery, Biography, History, or the Weather Channels, apply what they have read, and question or discuss what they are seeing.

Students must learn to read in different ways depending on the text, but good readers do some things consistently regardless of the text they are reading. In general, good readers:

- **Make connections**—Good readers think about what they read and relate it to their own lives and experiences by connecting it to prior knowledge. Readers pay more attention to what they are reading when they can relate personally to the text. They comprehend better when they think about the connections they make between the text, their lives, and the larger world. They look for similarities between the descriptions in the text and what they have experienced personally, heard about the world, or read in another text.

- **Ask questions**—Questioning is the strategy that keeps good readers engaged. When readers ask questions, they clarify understanding and make meaning out of what they are reading. Good readers ask themselves lots of questions about what they are reading. Why is this event happening? What does this mean? Who says this is a good thing to do? Asking questions is at the heart of thoughtful reading.

- **Visualize**—Good readers create visual images in their minds based on the words they read in the text. The pictures they create enhance their understanding and help their brains remember what they are reading. They "see" the setting, characters, and events as they occur. They connect nonfiction events to their experience.

- **Draw inferences and predict**—Inferring requires good readers to take what they already know, gather clues from the text, and think ahead to make a judgment, discern a theme, or predict what is to come. Good readers wonder what is going to happen next, and they think about how things will turn out. They think ahead when they read and make guesses about what is happening so they can stay interested in what they are reading. They read on to see if their predictions were correct. In fiction, predictions are usually about future events or a character's thoughts, feelings, words, and actions. In non-fiction, predictions are usually about future events, people, places, and ideas.

- **Determine important ideas**—Good readers grasp essential ideas and important information when reading. Good readers are thoughtful readers and they are able to differentiate between less important ideas and key ideas that are central to the meaning of the text.

- **Synthesize information**—Good readers fit things together as they read and come to conclusions. They combine new information with existing knowledge to form an original idea or interpretation of what they are reading. Good readers think about what they are reading and form opinions. They review, sort, and sift through important information in order to gain new insights that might change the way they think. Good readers develop opinions about what they are reading.

- **Monitor comprehension and clarify**—Good readers know when they understand what they read and when they do not. They pull things together as they read to make sure that what they are reading makes sense. If it doesn't make sense, they have strategies to "fix up" problems in their understanding as the problems arise. They try to answer any questions they have by using prior knowledge, context clues, rereading, or other resources.

Because reading is an active process in which the reader must interact with the text, the following presents a brief overview of what good readers do before, while, and after they read.

What Good Readers Do Before They Read

Even before reading a selection, good readers start asking themselves questions and thinking about what they are going to read. They set a purpose for their reading, preview what they are going to read, and plan how they are going to read. Good readers ask themselves these kinds of questions:

- What do I need to know before I read this material?

- What do I already know about the topic?

- How is the text organized to help me?

- What is the reason I am reading this material?

- What is the author's reason for writing this material?

- Am I reading for my own pleasure?
  If so, I can read at whatever pace I choose.

- Am I reading for school? If so, I have to ask
  some different kinds of questions as I read.

- Does the title tell me what the reading is about?

- Are there pictures, graphs, maps, titles, headings,
  boldface, or italics that can help me?

- Can I create a graphic organizer that will
  help me organize what I am going to read
  in a way that I can understand?

Reproduce the Good Reader bookmark on page 138 and have students use it as they get ready to read.

GOOD READER BOOKMARK
While I read I ask myself these questions:

- How does this connect to what I know?
- How does what I am reading compare to what I thought I knew?
- Does what I am reading make sense? If it does not, what is it that I don't understand?
- Do I need to code the text and note what is important, what I don't understand, what I need to re-read?
- Do I need to mark important words or ideas by highlighting, underlining, sticky notes, or transparent tape?
- Do I need to go back and re-read all or part of the material?
- Do the pictures, charts, graphs, or other visual aids help me understand what I am reading or give me more information that I need to know?
- Do I agree with the way the problem was solved? Am I surprised about the information? Is the information believable? Have I seen or heard something like this before?
- Are there clues for me so I can predict what the story is about and the problems that the characters will face? What descriptions do I need to remember?
- What is the plot or theme?
- What mental pictures do I see?
- What connections can I make from this passage to others that we have read in class?
- Who or what is the story about?
- When and where does the story take place?
- How and why do the events happen?
- Is there a specific problem that is solved?
- Do I see words that I don't know?

What Good Readers Do As They Read

Just as they do before reading, good readers have conversations and movies in their minds while they read. They read with a purpose and look for information that relates to that purpose. They try to connect the new information to other things they have read, heard, or experienced. They make inferences throughout their reading based on the background knowledge that they, personally, have. They visualize in their minds what is happening in the text as they read. Many good readers create sketches, concept maps, diagrams, charts, outlines, or notes as they are in the process of reading. These are visual ways to create and retain images. The visuals also help them identify the important elements.

As they read, good readers build meaning and frequently make predictions about what is to come. They read selectively, continually making decisions about their reading (what not to read, what to reread, and so on). Good readers construct, revise, and question the meanings they make as they read. They question what they do not understand or what is confusing to them, and they identify ways to figure out what has

54   *How to Teach Reading . . .*

confused them. They draw upon, compare, and integrate prior knowledge with current material in the text. They think about the author's text, style, beliefs, and intentions. They monitor their understanding of the text, making adjustments in their reading as necessary.

Good readers try to determine the meaning of unfamiliar words and concepts in the text and they deal with inconsistencies or gaps *as they read*. They use context, syntax (the way a word functions in a sentence), and structural analysis of words to increase their vocabulary and to figure out new words. They evaluate the text's quality and value, and they react to the text both intellectually and emotionally. They try to identify, remember, and summarize major ideas for comprehension.

Good readers read different kinds of texts differently, so it is important for content area teachers to model and teach strategies on "how" to read in their particular subjects. Good readers use specific strategies for specific subjects. For example, when reading narrative text *(as in an English class)*, good readers pay attention to the plot, setting, and characters. When reading expository material, like text in social studies, math, or science classes, good readers frequently construct and revise summaries of what they have read.

For good readers, text processing occurs not only during reading, but also during breaks in reading, and then again, after the reading is finished. While they read, good readers stop and ask themselves these kinds of questions:

- How does this connect to what I know?

- How does what I am reading compare to what I thought I knew?

- Does what I am reading make sense?
  If it does not, what is it that I don't understand?

- Do I need to code the text and note what is important, what I don't understand, and what I need to reread?

- Do I need to mark important words or ideas
  with highlighting, underlining, sticky notes,
  or transparent tape?

- Do I need to go back and reread
  all or part of the material?

- Do the pictures, charts, graphs, or other visual aids
  help me understand what I am reading or give me
  more information that I need to know?

- Do I agree with the way the problem was solved?
  Am I surprised about the information?
  Is the information believable?
  Have I seen or heard something like this before?

- Are there clues for me so I can predict what the
  story is about and the problems that the characters
  will face? What descriptions do I need to remember?

- What is the plot or theme?

- What mental pictures do I see?

- What connections can I make from this passage
  to others that we have read in class?

- Who or what is the story about?

- When and where does the story take place?

- How and why do the events happen?

- Is there a specific problem that is solved?

- Do I see words that I don't know?

What Good Readers Do After They Read

After the reading is complete, good readers stop and reflect on what they have read. They identify things they have learned or are confused about, and they react to what they have read on an intellectual and emotional level. The goal of the good reader is to expand their base of prior knowledge and make connections to create new understandings. Good readers want to enlarge their vocabulary and thinking abilities, and be able to use the new learning in their thinking, writing, and talking.

After reading, good readers try to summarize main ideas and try to state them in their own words. They skim the text and often reread the material to be able to meet the purpose of the reading and create a summary, an outline, a concept map, etc. After they read, good readers stop and ask themselves these kinds of questions:

- Did I find the answers to the questions I needed to answer?

- Did I learn what I wanted to learn?

- Were there other questions that I found?

- Were there questions or problems I didn't find?

- What do I know now that I did not know before?

- What is the most surprising or interesting thing I read?

- What new terms, concepts, or vocabulary did I learn?

- What do I remember?

- How do I feel about what I have read?

- Does my graphic organizer (if any) make sense?

- Can I restate the main points in my own words?

- How can I apply what I just read to my schoolwork and my life?

- Is there a lesson or moral in the story?

Myths About Readers

Some commonly held beliefs about reading are really myths. As teachers develop an understanding of the attributes of a good reader, they need to be careful to consider these myths.

Myth One:
Good readers skip letters and words

Contrary to what most people think, good readers do, indeed, look at all of the words and almost all of the letters in words when they read. The brain expects certain letters to occur in sequence with other letters, so it seeks familiar letter patterns in words.

It is easy to assume that poor readers read slowly and choppily because they are looking at each word and letter, while good readers can read quickly because they skip words. This is not true.

Myth Two:
Hearing inner voices is bad

Good readers have an inner voice in their heads that they hear when they read. They hear words in their minds and this helps them create meaning as they read—different characters can even have different voices. It is easy to recognize students and adults who have not developed "inner voices" yet, because they move their lips or mumble as they read. Noticing this lack of inner voice is an important observation for middle grades teachers.

Have you ever instructed your class to read something silently and stood by as some of them proceed to read out loud in normal voices? When students did that in

How to Teach Reading . . .

*my class, I would say, "Class, remember you are to read this paragraph **silently**." The students who had been reading out loud would look up at me like I was crazy for reminding them. I finally realized that these students had simply not developed their inner voices and had to read out loud so they could hear themselves and think about what they were reading.*

Here are ways to deal with students who do not hear inner voices:

• *Change the way questions are asked.*

Students who do not have inner voices tend to blurt out answers during discussions. Teach students that when a question is asked, no one is to blurt out an answer immediately. Instead, students should quickly turn to a neighbor and ask the same question of each other. When the pair is finished, they turn their attention back to the teacher, who then calls on one student to answer the question for the entire class. This process takes only a few minutes and accomplishes several things. First, the kids with no inner voices get to blurt at another student. *(This way, they still get to hear themselves think.)* Second, all the kids get to share their answers before sharing them with the class and very often a kid who is clueless gets to hear an answer that is at least on the topic from another student. Most importantly, this format eliminates competition for the teacher's attention between the blurters and the hand-wavers. All students get to contribute answers whether they are correct or not.

Do not worry that students occasionally hear incorrect information using this technique. Remember, this is a management technique for kids who do not have an inner voice and who blurt out their thoughts all the time, not a Think, Pair, Share activity!

- ***Get them on the phone!***
Buy PVC elbows and make "phones" for students. When students are reading silently in class, ask them to whisper to themselves using the phones. This keeps class noise to a minimum, and students still get to hear themselves read. Take it a step further and turn the mouth- and earpieces outward so that two kids can read together—one reads while the other one listens and then they can switch. This works well and the kids love it.

Myth Three: Good readers always use context

Most good readers recognize common words quickly and automatically without using context. Context is used only after the brain has processed the word letter-by-letter. When students do not know a word, some teachers tell them to "sound it out" and then figure out what it means by using the context. Poor readers do not know the letter sounds and do not have the experiences necessary to interpret the context. They have almost no chance of figuring out new words.

Good readers can self-correct their misreading because they are able to use context; poor readers cannot. Good self-correctors effectively use semantics (word meaning), syntax (how the word is used in the sentence), and their knowledge of letter-sound relationships. Therefore, telling a poor reader they must use the context to figure out a word is not likely to work.

Myth Four:
Spelling patterns help all readers decode new words

The brain recognizes familiar spelling patterns, or words with similar patterns, that the reader has in memory. Good readers use spelling patterns and words they already know to help them understand new words. However, poor readers probably do not have enough words in their reading vocabulary memory to recognize spelling patterns.

Good readers figure out big words by "chunking" them into manageable parts. They look for familiar parts of old words inside the new words. As Patricia Cunningham says,

> In order to use known words to figure out big words, you must know some big words. Not only must you be able to read some big words, but you must also be able to spell those big words. The requirement that you be able to spell some big words along with the tendency of readers to guess or skip any word of more than seven letters may partially explain why so many older children experience problems reading their content-area texts.

Poor readers just do not have the vocabulary reservoir to figure out big words.

CHAPTER 4

READING STRATEGIES

"...effective teachers are able to craft a special mix of instructional
ingredients for every child they work with...there is a common
menu of materials, strategies, and environments from which
effective teachers make choices...as a society, our most important
challenge is to make sure that our teachers have access to those
tools and the knowledge required to use them well."

— *"Preventing Reading Difficulties in Young Children"*
National Research Council, pg. 3

Strategies for Teaching Comprehension

Before their students ever read anything, most teachers begin by giving the students background knowledge and preparing them for what they are going to read. Teachers often go to great lengths to make the material interesting enough to grab students' attention and motivate them to read the selection. Unfortunately, this tactic often gets students to read just enough so they will pass a test on the information. Obviously, this practice does not always encourage student comprehension and critical thinking about the content.

Research has identified strategies that are effective when helping students develop comprehension skills and that improve student understanding. These strategies can be used at any grade level or for any subject. Tierney and Readence (2000) summarize the benefits of using these strategies.

They will increase student-text interaction and comprehension and are designed to help teachers:

- activate students' prior knowledge
- foster active and engaged reading
- guide students' reading of a text
- reinforce concepts gleaned from the text reading
- encourage careful/critical thinking when reading a text
- pursue inquiry on different topics

As teachers select reading strategies for their classrooms, they should remember that middle grades students require active learning. They need to do more than worksheets. Further, all students have different personalities and learning styles, so classroom activities should be varied. Middle School students come to class with many different levels of word knowledge, so strategies must fit a variety of levels at one time. Teachers must create ways that students can associate vocabulary with something meaningful, so that students can do more than just memorize words, formulas, or concepts. Once these connections are made, it will be more likely they will be remembered. After the new content is associated with meaning, there must be practice with the content. It is necessary to provide visual, auditory, and kinesthetic ways for students to learn and remember content-specific words and concepts.

Choose the strategies that fit your needs from those explained in this chapter. Modify them to fit your specific content needs. All of the strategies are easy to incorporate in classrooms; they start working immediately to help students read with better comprehension; and they are good choices for content area teachers new to the teaching of reading.

> "Children who don't know what reading and writing are
> for in the real world do not have the same drive and
> motivation as children for whom reading and writing,
> like eating and sleeping, are things everyone does."
>
> —*Cunningham*

READING STRATEGY 1—*Learning Walls*

Learning walls provide:

- a way for students to associate meaning with the words

- practice using a variety of learning modes

Some middle grades teachers, when first hearing about learning walls, think "how elementary-schoolish!" and worry that it sounds too much like being forced to have pretty bulletin boards. *Who has time to waste decorating a classroom when there are curriculum guides to cover, standards to be met, and state tests to address?*

How to Teach Reading . . .

The research about learning and the importance of brain-based instruction points out that the power of visualization is a part of long-term memory *(and a reading strategy).* Any teacher who has posted a relevant chart or a graph on a classroom wall—and has then removed it for a test—has seen how students will look at the blank space as if the chart were still there. These students are "recreating" the information in their memories simply by glancing at the spot where the chart used to be.

At the beginning of the school year, generate a list of essential words, concepts, formulas, or whatever students must know in a particular content area. This list of essentials is the perfect place to begin a word wall. Create charts showing the information, and place them in a prominent place in the classroom where students will be exposed to them before, during, and after being introduced to the content. The basic learning wall is in place.

Once a learning wall is set up, teachers will notice that their students use it as they are reading and writing. Enhance the learning wall with color, location, and pattern as recommended in brain-based research. Refer to the wall often. Help students connect new concepts with the information on the wall. *(Then, just like the athletic skills that become automatic with practice, the recognition of essential content becomes automatic.)* Students will have an "accessible dictionary" on the wall and since the recognition of the words in this dictionary has become automatic, they are ready to use the words as they read and write.

Selecting a Location for the Learning Wall

Learning walls are not simply fancy bulletin boards, they are an important part of the learning process. Take advantage of the physical attributes of the classrooms. Use whatever is available—desks, doors, cabinets, windows, ceilings, blinds, light fixtures, bookcases—to create a learning wall.

Put the learning wall anywhere the kids can see it. Add pictures and phrases to the learning wall so students can look for *(and find)* patterns. Some teachers use file folders as *"portable learning walls"* students can keep at their desks.

Teachers should start simply when creating learning walls. Using 4" x 6" index cards, write the words on them and stick them on the wall. For larger images, charts, or lists, use laminated and colored paper. Try using the same color for words that share the same concept; change to another color when the theme, chapter, or area of study changes. After all, since research has shown that the brain thinks in color, location, pattern, and odd numbers, teachers should make use of these features and give students access to all of them!

Selecting Words, Formulas, and Concepts for the Learning Wall

According to Cunningham (1999), these are critical elements for using a learning wall:

- Be selective and include only essential words, formulas, or concepts that students need for your topic or subject.

- Add words gradually—about five words a week.

- Make words accessible by putting them where everyone can see them; use big black letters and/or different colors.

- Practice the words daily by chanting, writing, and moving. Students can't just look at and remember the words.

- Make sure learning wall words are spelled correctly in all student work.

- Do a variety of review activities to provide practice until the words are read and spelled instantly and automatically.

Select words that students will see and use often in reading and writing in your content area. Make sure to tell students that all of the words on the learning wall are important because they will see them over and over again, and that the terms will help them in their reading and their writing. Give the students an example of one of the words that is important because it shares with others the same suffix or root, and then add or explain three more words or terms that have the same pattern. As words change with different prefixes or suffixes, note how the root word changes meaning.

DID YOU KNOW?

Black ink on yellow paper stimulates learning.

Making the Learning Wall Interactive

The more times a teacher is able to refer to the words on the learning wall, the more powerful it becomes as a visualization tool for long-term memory. Try to include an activity or comment about the words on the learning wall every day and have the students use the information. The more they use the words, the more they will retain them.

Here are two interactive ways to use a learning wall:

Guess the Word

This activity takes little pre-planning and is a great warm-up activity at the beginning of class to get students settled and on task.

Choose a word, formula, concept, and so forth, from the learning wall. Have students write the numbers one through five on a blank sheet of paper. Give five clues. After each clue, students write their guesses by the number of the clue. By the fifth clue, everyone should have guessed the word. The first clue is always the same: "It's one of the words on the learning wall."

Each clue will narrow down the possibilities until only one word will work. Decide what students need to remember about the word and make the clues focus on that understanding. One possible format for the five clues follows.

- •Clue 1: It's one of the words on the learning wall from this chapter.

- • Clue 2: It has ____ syllables.

- • Clue 3: It's used only when . . .

- • Clue 4: It's part of . . .

- • Clue 5: It completes the sentence . . .

Wordo

A spin-off of Bingo or Lotto, this is a good test review game.

Make Wordo game sheets with the number of empty squares depending on the number of words you have displayed. Don't forget the "free space" in the middle. If possible, laminate the blank sheets so they can be reused. Give students blank Wordo game sheets and have them write a different word from the learning wall into each of the blank boxes. *This way every card will be unique.*

Give students objects (such as beans or pennies) to cover the words. As you call out the words one at a time, the students cover the words on their cards. The first one to cover a row, four corners, or the whole card, wins. Make the game harder. Require students to provide a definition of each word as it is called back. *This encourages them to choose words from the wall that they know.*

Wordo Grid

FREE

How to Teach Reading When You're Not a Reading Teacher
Copyright ©2006 by Incentive Publications, Inc., Nashville, TN
139

How to Teach Reading . . .

READING STRATEGY 2—*Sorts*

Sorting is a wonderful activity to develop spelling, vocabulary, and comprehension skills. It works because students actively become involved in how words, processes, formulas, and concepts are connected within the content. In classes where sorts are used regularly, students look forward to learning new words and begin thinking about where they fit with what they already know. As students manipulate words, they learn to use what they know about them and make new connections that transfer to their reading and writing.

Teachers can differentiate instruction by using multi-level sorts on the same concept. Simply form groups of different students to focus on sets of different, *and appropriate*, words. Sorts can be done with words from the learning wall or any group of terms, words, or information that students need to memorize, label, or categorize.

How to Do a Sort

1. First, decide the purpose of the sort. Is it to introduce new words or concepts or is it to be used as a review before a test?

2. Next write 10–15 words, formulas, and so forth, on index cards or strips of paper.

3. Have students sort the cards into different piles, depending on the criteria given them. It could be by term-definition, how the terms are alike or different, alphabetically, numerically, sequentially, chronologically—whatever works best for the content.

   Hints: Use self-closing plastic bags to store word cards. Make enough sets for students to work in pairs or individually. At times, teachers should allow students to determine which type of sort they choose to do. Students make some of the best sorts! Once again, if this process works well, start laminating and using colors.

Some Sorts to Consider

• Open Sort

The teacher provides only the words, and students decide the sort categories based on the words they have. Open sorts are valuable because they allow the teacher to see what students know and understand.

• Closed Sort

The teacher provides the categories for the sort. Closed sorts are used more frequently than open sorts because they allow the teacher to focus the students' attention on a feature, characteristic, pattern, or concept that the class is studying.

Closed sorts are valuable assessment tools because the teacher can rapidly assess student understanding by checking students' sorts for correctness.

• Speed Sort

A speed sort is a timed sort students can do once they are adept at sorting. Speed sorts are excellent for building fluency and accuracy when working with well-known patterns and concepts. Students can record the time it takes to sort and then try to beat their own records.

• Blind Sort

This is an auditory closed sort in which the teacher calls out the words. The students point to or say the categories they see listed on the worksheet, board, or overhead. Blind sorts are useful when the teacher wants to focus on sound patterns rather than visual patterns.

• Writing Sort

The students have a sorting card with key words written as column headers. They write words under the appropriate categories as the teacher calls them out, using the key words as spelling guides. Writing sorts focus on auditory and visual patterns in words and combine both aspects of closed and blind sorts.

READING STRATEGY 3—Think Alouds

This strategy models for students how to connect what they know to the text they are reading. The teacher reads aloud from a text, stopping after a short passage, then "thinks aloud," demonstrating how to make connections that lead to better comprehension of the text. The only difficult part of this strategy for some teachers is that they are not used to "thinking about how they think," so explaining this to students is not an easy task.

Although most teachers plan think alouds, they seem spontaneous to students. Think alouds are an important part of teaching any comprehension strategy to students. This metacognition is a way of helping students monitor and improve their own comprehension.

In a Think Aloud, teachers model strategies for solving problems as they read. Readers can run into all kinds of comprehension problems in a text, so a teacher simulates a comprehension problem and thinks aloud how the problem can be solved, showing students what to do when something is hard to understand.

Here are a few trouble-shooting techniques that are important to model for students :

1. Keep reading to see if the author explains what you don't understand.
2. Reread to see if you missed something.
3. Read back to the part you didn't understand, or, read forward skipping confusing words.
4. Reflect on what you have read and see if there is an alternative explanation that can be inferred based on your prior knowledge.
5. Seek information beyond the text (from a partner or a second source) in order to understand.

Teachers need to encourage students to do think alouds themselves when they read. As students think aloud, the teacher can monitor their understanding as well as observe their reasoning. Think alouds can easily be nested within any instruction, and they tend to make a teacher's oral reading exercises more engaging and understandable for all students.

READING STRATEGY 4—KWL, KWHL, KWWL Charts

The KWL strategy (Ogle, 1986) provides a framework to help readers access knowledge about a topic before they read, consider what they want to learn, and then record what they have learned once they finish reading. It helps students reinforce the comprehension skills of questioning, predicting, clarifying, and summarizing. It also helps students focus on how they will learn the content. Using the graphic organizer helps transfer information to long-term memory.

Many teachers incorporate this strategy, but it has become more of a worksheet or demonstration that is quickly put on the board rather than a focused comprehension tool. When using a KWL, teach the strategy first and make sure students understand the significance of the steps and how they impact comprehension.

- **K** stands for **Know—**
  What do I already know about this topic? Before reading, students fill in this column to activate prior knowledge. (If they do not know anything about this topic, this is not a good strategy to use for this type of reading.)

- **W** stands for **Will** or **Want—**
  What do I think I will learn about this topic? What will I want to know about this topic? Students make a prediction based on a quick preview of the text to be read. Use titles, headings, bold and italicized words, pictures, charts, graphs, as clues to set the purpose for the reading and focus on key ideas. This step helps students generate questions about the knowledge, and then read to answer those questions.

- **L** stands for **Learned—**
  What have I learned about this topic? After reading, students fill in the knowledge they gained from the content. This is a time to correct misperceptions or incorrect information about the topic. This might be considered the metacognition or "Think Aloud" stage.

Many variations of KWL may be used. Consider adding columns for:

- **H** stands for **How**—
  How do I find the information? This column can be used by students who need to use a process or formula to comprehend the content.

- **W** stands for **Where**—
  Where do I find the information? This column is good because it allows students to brainstorm different sources of information at their disposal.

READING STRATEGY 5—Anticipation Guides

This strategy, developed by Tierney, Readence, and Dishner, is used before, during, and after reading. This strategy works best when students have limited knowledge of a topic.

- **Preparing for the Activity**—The teacher develops three to five statements that address issues related to the major topics or themes of the text. Reproduce one anticipation guide (form on page 144), write the statements on the guide, and then reproduce the statements for students. Make sure the statements present important generalizations about the issues that are worth discussing, but do not have clear-cut answers. Statements should be debatable and experience-based.

- **Pre-reading Discussion**—Distribute the anticipation guide and have students decide whether they agree or disagree with each statement. Briefly discuss their opinions. This will activate students' prior knowledge, encourage them to make personal connections to what they will be reading, and give them a chance to become active participants with the text before they begin reading.

- **Reading with Purpose**—As students read, they take notes on the statements. Encourage students to read critically and try to understand the issues with an open mind or from different points of view.

- **Post-Reading Discussion**—Review students' original responses and see if they have changed their thinking. Ask such questions as:

  1. Did we find answers to our questions?
  2. What questions do we still have?
  3. What information did we learn that we did not anticipate before we read?
  4. What have we learned by reading this selection?
  5. What was the most interesting, unusual, or surprising information you learned?

The post-reading discussion gives the teacher a quick assessment of how well the students understood the text.

How to Teach Reading . . .

READING STRATEGY 6—*PIC:*
Purpose — Important Ideas — Connections

This strategy is used before reading to help students activate background knowledge by previewing the text. It helps students focus on the most important information and allows them to make predictions and generate questions before they read. The goal is for students to establish a purpose for reading and to remember what they have read when they are finished. Reproduce the PIC form on page 145 for students. Model this strategy in a "think aloud" before expecting students to use the strategy independently.

- P stands for Purpose:
  What is my purpose for reading? What am I going to do with the information when I finish reading? Will I write a paper, take a test, do a graphic organizer, do a project?

- I stands for Important Ideas:
  How can I determine what important ideas are in the reading? Have students preview the text. Look at the title, pictures, headings, bold or italicized print, charts, graphs, maps, and sidebar sections. Is there anything in the table of contents, index, or glossary that can help me get the big idea? Are there questions to guide me in the reading? What are the key words I need to know?

- C stands for Connection:
  What do I already know about this subject? How does it fit with what I have already learned? What questions do I want answered? What does this remind me of? What questions would I like to have answered by the text?

After students read, have them go back and see if their predictions were accurate, if their questions were answered, and if they understood the important ideas based on their preview of the text features.

Reproduce this page at 120% for 8½ x 11 size. Use it with the strategy on page 77.

PIC Form

P	I	C
Put your **PURPOSE** for reading here	Write three or four **IMPORTANT IDEAS**, words, or concepts here	Write how what you already knew about the subject **CONNECTED** with what you learned

PIC Form

P	I	C
Put your **PURPOSE** for reading here	Write three or four **IMPORTANT IDEAS**, words, or concepts here	Write how what you already knew about the subject **CONNECTED** with what you learned

How to Teach Reading When You're Not a Reading Teacher
Copyright ©2006 by Incentive Publications, Inc., Nashville, TN   145

READING STRATEGY 7—*3–2–1*

This strategy requires students to summarize key ideas, rethink these ideas in order to focus on information they found interesting or difficult to understand, and then ask one question about what they still want to know.

Students complete the 3–2–1 strategy chart with the following information:

- **3** key ideas I found out from the reading
- **2** things that were especially interesting or especially hard to understand
- **1** question I still have

This format can be used in a variety of ways. Students might complete the chart using this formula:

- **3** differences between _____ and _____
- **2** similarities between them
- **1** question I still have

The format can be modified to fit the content being taught. This strategy is beneficial because it is brain-compatible (containing odd numbers and small chunks of information). It is a simple way to get students to differentiate between important and unimportant details.

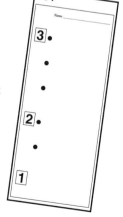

Reproduce the 3-2-1 chart (page 146) for students. When the forms are completed, use student responses to construct an outline, complete a graphic organizer, identify sequence, or isolate cause and effect. Student responses can form the basis for class discussion of the reading. The students are motivated because the discussion is based on the ideas that they found and consider important. This strategy encourages them to make a personal connection to what they have read.

How to Teach Reading . . .

READING STRATEGY 8—RAFT

The acronym in this post-reading strategy stands for Role, Audience, Format, Topic (Vandervanter and Adler, 1982). This strategy gives students a structured way to format written responses to reading. It also allows them to be more creative in their responses.

Reproduce the RAFT planning sheet (page 147) or simply have students record answers on a blank paper. Students assume a role, identify the audience, choose a format, and pick a topic before they begin their response.

- **Role of the Writer**

  Who are you as the writer? A famous person? A character from the reading? A concerned citizen? A reporter?

- **Audience**

  Think about your audience. To whom are you writing? Is your audience a friend? Your teacher? Readers of a newspaper?

- **Format**

  Consider your purpose, then choose a format. Will your writing persuade, entertain, describe, or inform? What form will the writing take? Is it a letter? A speech? A classified ad? A poem? A help column? A persuasive essay?

- **Topic**

  What is your topic? Write a good topic sentence here.

RAFT Planning Sheet

Role of the Writer	Who are you as the writer? A famous person? A character from the reading? A concerned citizen? A reporter?	
Audience	Think about your audience. To whom are you writing? Is your audience a friend? Your teacher? Readers of a newspaper?	
Format	Consider your purpose, then choose a format. Will your writing persuade, entertain, describe, or inform? What form will the writing take? Is it a letter? A speech? A classified ad? A poem? A help column? A persuasive essay?	
Topic	What is your topic? Write a good topic sentence here.	

READING STRATEGY 9—*More Graphic Organizers*

A graphic organizer is a visual representation that shows how key concepts are related. Graphic organizers help students visualize connections between ideas. They can be called any number of names such as pictorial organizers, webs, maps, diagrams, but all are visual ways to represent information. When selecting the right graphic organizer consider the structure of the text. Then use the organizer to help students understand and remember information.

The advantages of using graphic organizers to help students in the various content areas are:

- Once students have picked out the important ideas, there is little to reread.

- They provide a way to organize content for better recall and understanding.

- They help kids "see" more abstract content, and technical terms can be taught in clusters to show connections.

- They are easy to construct and discuss.

- Students can create their own.

Any piece of text can be displayed in more than one way depending on the purpose for reading. Graphic organizers can be used for planning, note taking, organizing, drawing conclusions, or assessing.

Present different graphic organizers to students and evaluate their usefulness together. Students will learn to choose for themselves which type of organizer best suits the structure of a particular text they are reading.

Eventually, students will create and use their own graphic organizers. They can read, take notes, and then work in groups to create a graphic organizer to share with the class.

Graphic organizers help student visualize information in a variety of ways:

- by main idea, sub-topics, and details

- in sequence

How to Teach Reading . . .

- to show relationships between different parts
- by components like the elements in a story
- by similarities and differences
- by cause and effect
- by stages of a process

Here are several examples of graphic organizer formats:

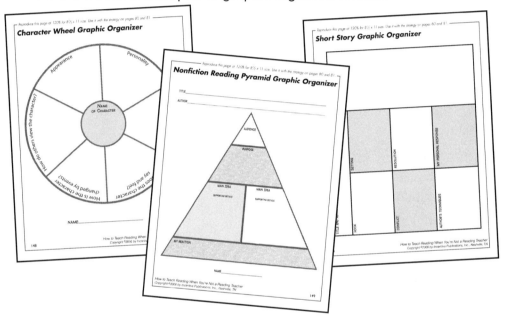

READING STRATEGY 10—*Column Notes*

The column note format, based on the Cornell Note Taking System, has many variations. Change the column headings to fit the objective and material being read. Column notes are best used when teaching advanced comprehension skills like cause and effect and comparison and contrast. Information is grouped according to type, then arranged in columns. Two-column notes are the easiest because students can fold the paper down the middle to create the columns. The number of columns can be increased depending on the type of information and the purpose of the notes.

For example, students can make column notes with:

- main ideas or headings and details or explanations
- cause and effect
- vocabulary and definitions
- questions and answers
- facts and opinions
- predictions and outcomes

Some teachers find it useful to expand to three columns. Example headings for three columns might include (but certainly are not limited to):

- vocabulary—definition—example
- topic—explanation—supporting details
- process—procedure—results
- questions—notes from reading—class discussion
- cause—effect—explanation

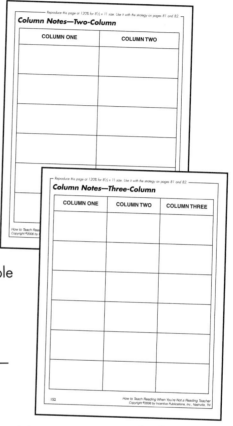

The column note format is handy, and the organization of information is clear and visually useful for students.

READING STRATEGY 11—*QAR: Question-Answer Relationships*

The QAR strategy (Raphael, 1982, 1986) provides students with a process to find and support an answer to a question. QAR encourages students to be strategic about their search for answers based on the relationship between the questions asked and the expected answers. Teach this strategy early in the year so students will learn how to generate different levels of questions as they are reading.

There are four types of Question-Answer Relationships. The first two questions are literal *(in the text)*, and the second two questions are inferential *(in the students' heads)* and require prior knowledge.

1. **Right There**—The answer is usually contained in a single sentence in the text, and the words in the question are often the same words in the text. The answer is "right there." *(I always point!)* **Right There** questions begin with words like "Who is," "What is," "How many," or "Name." The answer is usually one word or a short phrase, and there is only one correct answer. Sample questions are: "In what year did Columbus discover America?" or "Who was the sixteenth president?"

2. **Think and Search**—The answer is in the text, but it may require looking in several sentences to find it. The reader must "search" for the answer like a detective and "think" about how the information or ideas in the text relate to each other. **Think and Search** questions begin with words or statements like, "Summarize," "Retell," "Compare," "Explain," or "Find three examples." A sample **Think and Search** question is: "Compare the functions of a plant's roots to the functions of a plant's stem."

3. **Author and You**—The answer is not in the text, but the reader must have read the text to answer the question. Readers will use information that the author has given combined with prior knowledge, in order to answer the question. A sample question is: "The reading was about life in the eighteenth century. How does life today differ from life then?"

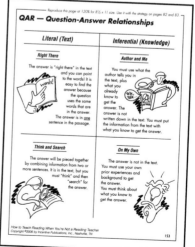

4. **On My Own**—The answer is not in the text, and in fact, reading the text is not even necessary to answer the question. This response is based on the reader's personal beliefs and prior knowledge.

READING STRATEGY 12—*Visual Reading Guides*

This strategy (Stein, 1978) is used to preview the selection to be read by noting the visuals provided in the text. Teachers help students identify important visual aids like maps, charts, graphs, pictures, cartoons, and so forth, that relate to the content or main ideas of the text. Visual reading guides help students understand the features of nonfiction text. Depending on the purpose of the reading, students learn to evaluate visuals based on their importance and quality. The teacher should model a think aloud to help students with questions such as:

- How is the visual information related to the text?

- Why did the author include the visual?

- What does the visual show me?

- How is the visual organized?

- How can I use the information from the visual to help me understand what I'm going to read?

- Why is the information from the visual important to the text?

After the teacher does the think aloud, students should list two or three questions that arise from the visual aids and predict their importance to understanding what they will be reading. After the reading, students review the visual aids and decide if they did or did not provide important information.

A bookmark with the acronym for a strategy that has been taught is a handy reminder for students. Reproduce and use these bookmarks (page 156) and their acronyms or create your own.

RIDER: A Visual Imagery Strategy

R   Read the sentence.
I   Imagine a picture of it in your mind.
D   Describe how the new image differs from the old.
E   Evaluate to see that the image contains everything.
R   Repeat as you read the next sentence.

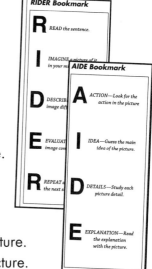

AIDE: Strategy for Picture Interpretation

A   Action—Look for the action in the picture.
I   Idea—Guess the main idea of the picture.
D   Details—Study each picture detail.
E   Explanation—Read the explanation with the picture.

READING STRATEGY 13—Vocabulary/Concept Maps

Several mapping strategies were introduced during the 1970s and 1980s that help students acquire vocabulary and concept knowledge. These strategies are a good alternative to the practice many teachers had of simply teaching and testing students on word definitions.

Using vocabulary/concept maps builds on students' prior knowledge to help them see relationships with new words, terms, or concepts. In this way, students develop related—*rather than isolated*—word knowledge and skill in differentiating concepts, as well as defining words. Each mapping strategy can be used before, during, and after reading, depending on the emphasis of the learning.

Four examples of vocabulary concept maps are explained below.

Semantic Mapping *(JOHNSON AND PEARSON, 1978)*

A semantic map, sometimes called a spider diagram or a semantic web, is a diagram with a key concept at the center and related concepts placed at the ends of radiating spokes. It is to make and show the connections between word meanings. Semantic maps help students organize what they know, so the words become more meaningful and memorable.

Semantic mapping can be used before or after reading, either to activate prior knowledge or to organize the new words that are learned. Stahl (1999) drew the following conclusions about the effectiveness of semantic mapping:

- Semantic mapping can improve word knowledge.

- Semantic mapping can improve comprehension of material containing the words included in the map.

- Group maps made by the students are more effective than provided ready-made maps.

- Poor readers benefit greatly from semantic maps.

Here are step-by-step directions for creating a semantic map:

1. Present a concept to students and have them brainstorm words that are related to the concept or topic being studied.

2. List their words, then add words students did not include.

3. Work with the students to develop definitions of the new words.

4. Place the target concept at the center of a diagram.

5. Get related key words and concepts from the students' list and place them radiating out from the central concept, grouping them into related

categories. Make sure that a key concept anchors the end of each spoke and then draw a box or oval around it.

6. Introduce new words and related concepts attached to those known by students.

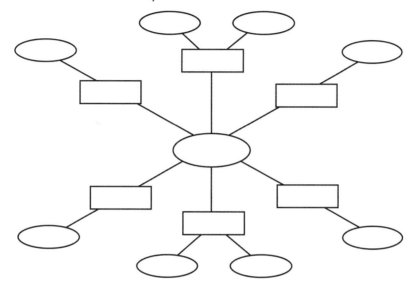

Semantic Feature Analysis *(JOHNSON AND PEARSON, 1978)*

1. Select a category of related terms.

2. List terms in a column.

3. List features (characteristics) to be explored in rows above the terms.

4. Indicate feature possession with + or –, or scale 1–3.

5. Explore new terms and/or features through discussion.

	Characteristic 1	Characteristic 2	Characteristic 3	Characteristic 4
Term 1	+	–	–	+
Term 2	–	–	–	+
Term 3	+	+	+	–
Term 4	–	+	+	–
Term 5	–	+	–	+

Word Concept or
Word Definition Mapping *(SCHWARTZ AND RAPHAEL, 1985)*

1. Identify a target word or concept.

2. Guide students to identify relevant (essential) characteristics and contrast these with irrelevant (nonessential) characteristics.

3. Generate examples to illustrate concept.

4. Attach concept to a larger category.

5. Consider related but different concepts within this category.

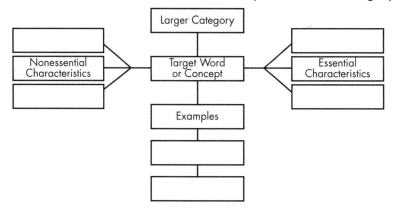

DISSECT Method for Vocabulary

D   discover the context
I   isolate the prefix
S   separate the suffix
S   say the stem
E   examine the stem
C   check with someone
T   try the dictionary or thesaurus

READING STRATEGY 14—*Questioning the Author*

This was a strategy designed by McKeown, Beck, and Worthy in 1993. Questioning the Author is used to help students think beyond the words on the page and to consider the author's purpose and effectiveness. Students are looking at the author's intent, clarity, and organization.

After reading a selection, students answer five questions:

1. What is the author trying to tell you?
2. Why is the author telling you that?
3. Does the author say it clearly?
4. How could the author have said things more clearly?
5. What would you say instead?

According to McKeown et al., students should read text with a "reviser's eye." Sometimes when students have trouble understanding text, they assume it is because they are poor readers. McKeown et al., see the idea of the "fallible author" and want students not to quit reading when the text becomes difficult, but instead to analyze what the author has done to make it so difficult for the reader.

READING STRATEGY 15—*Reciprocal Teaching*

This strategy (Palincsar et al., 1984, 1986) is a compilation of four comprehension strategies: summarizing, questioning, clarifying, and predicting. Students need to have used all four strategies individually before they try this one.

One way to use this strategy is to have students read with a four-column chart. Each column is labeled for a comprehension strategy. Students make notes in each category.

Another approach is to put students in groups of four and assign each one a role: summarizer, questioner, clarifier, and predictor. Students assume their roles, read a few paragraphs of the selection, take notes, and underline or use notes to highlight key information. When they stop at a given point, the summarizer will give the major points; the questioner will ask questions about unclear parts, puzzling information, or new words; the clarifier will address the confusing parts and try to answer the questions; and the predictor will guess what will happen next or what will be learned as they read.

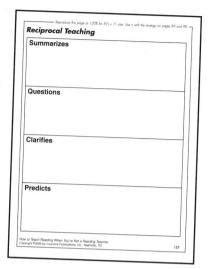

Divide a reading into four sections, switch roles four times, and each student will have a chance to play all four roles.

READING STRATEGY 16—*ABC Brainstorming*

This simple strategy can be used before, during, or after reading. Students brainstorm a word or phrase associated with the topic to match with each letter of the alphabet.

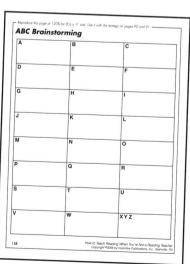

- Before studying a major topic, use this strategy to check background knowledge.

- During the reading, it can be used as a way to summarize what students have learned to a certain point.

- After reading, it can be used to create a summary or a review of the knowledge gained. It is most useful when the topic is broad enough so that students can generate many possible terms.

Step-by Step Directions

1. Have students list the letters of the alphabet down a sheet of paper or reproduce the form on page 158 with the alphabet in boxes.

2. In no particular order, have students fill in words or phrases beside each letter.

3. Let students work individually at the beginning to give them plenty of time to think.

4. After they brainstorm alone, put them in pairs or small groups to compare answers and fill in any letters that were left blank.

5. Have students share their answers with the class.

6. At the end of the ABC Brainstorming, either have students write a summary paragraph of what they think are the major points, or have them create a graphic organizer of what they learned.

READING STRATEGY 17—Signal Words

Good readers adjust how they read text based on their purpose for reading. Signal words tell the reader the structure of the text so they will know how to think as they are reading. The clues will help them analyze the text and think clearly about what it is saying. Signal words help students predict, clarify, and question. They tell what is coming and what to watch for in the reading. Watching for signal words will focus the readers' attention and make them note the information to follow.

Students preview the text and look for signal words. They should generate a list, then discuss what they think the structure of the text will be. Students should be asking themselves:

- What kind of thinking will I need to do to understand the text?

- Which of the text structures is being used?

- How can I display the information after I read?

• What kind of graphic organizer can I create to visualize and connect the information?

Students discuss and determine a structure (cause and effect, description, etc.), then write one sentence about what they think the main idea may be.

After reading, students check their predictions and use a graphic organizer, write a summary, or in some way organize what they have learned.

Here are six common structures and a suggestion of a graphic organizer for each:

Five W's and How

Signal Words: **Who, What, When, Where, Why,** and **How**

These are the most commonly used signal words. Learning them is a great way to introduce signal words, because these are the questions that good reporters or detectives always ask to get the most important details. Try drawing these on the fingers of a hand with "how" on the palm. Or say "Give me five," and the kids know to answer "The five W's and how."

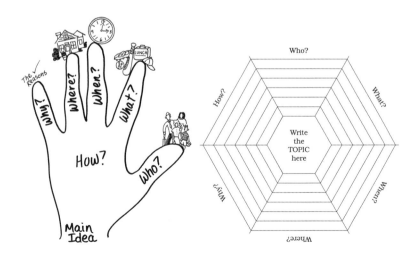

How to Teach Reading . . .

Cause and Effect

Signal Words: *because, therefore, consequently, this led to, If . . . then, nevertheless, since, so, in order to, accordingly, because of, as a result of, may be due to, for this reason, not only . . . but, so that,* and *thus.*

Compare and Contrast

Signal Words: *different from, same as, similar to, as opposed to, instead of, although, however, compared with, as well as, either . . . or, but, on the other hand, unless, not only . . . but also, while, yet, but,* and *unlike.*

Description, Problem, and Solution

Signal Words: *the question is, a solution, problem, one answer is,* and any of the signal words from cause and effect.

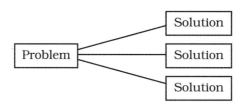

Description and Enumeration

Signal Words: *for instance, to illustrate, for example, such as, in addition, another, most importantly, furthermore, first, second, to begin with, then, in fact, several, numerous, also, many, and few.*

Items needed for camping:

1.

2.

3.

4.

5.

6.

7.

Sequence or Chronological Order

Signal Words: *not long after, next, then, initially, before, after, finally, proceeding, following, over the years, today, when, on (date), now, and gradually.*

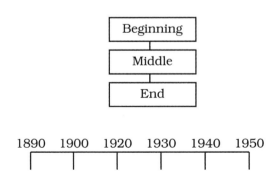

READING STRATEGY 18—SCAMPER

SCAMPER is a mnemonic device developed by Eberle to help students expand their thinking during brainstorming. It is a systematic way for students to generate new ideas or modify existing ones to encourage creative thinking. This strategy works especially well after reading.

S—Substitute
Substitute something new in the passage to take the place of a character, event, location, time, etc.
Have a thing or person act or serve in another's place.

C—Combine
Combine purposes, ideas, materials from the story.
Bring together or unite.

A—Adapt
Adjust to suit a condition, tune up or down, agree, reshape.
(How would the story change if it were set in modern times?)

M—Modify—Alter or change in form or quality.
Magnify—Enlarge or make greater in quality or form.
Minify—Make smaller, lighter, slower, less frequent.

P—Put to other uses
Use for a purpose other than originally intended.

E—Eliminate
Remove, omit, simplify, or get rid of a quality, part, or whole.

R—Reverse or Rearrange
Change order or sequence, adjust, create another layout or scheme.

Reproduce this page at 120% for 8½ x 11 size. Use it with the strategy on page 95.

SCAMPER

S
Substitute

C
Combine

A
Adapt

M
Modify

P
Put to other uses

E
Eliminate

R
Reverse or Rearrange

How to Teach Reading When You're Not a Reading Teacher
Copyright ©2006 by Incentive Publications, Inc., Nashville, TN

159

READING STRATEGY 19—SQ3R Reading Strategy

SQ3R is an acronym for the five steps that comprise a comprehensive reading strategy that has been around for years. It is not a difficult strategy to teach, and it helps students think about the material before, during, and after they read. The basic steps are:

S—Survey the reading material to get an idea about the nature of the content. Determine the structure, organization, or plan of the text. Details will be remembered because of their relationship to the total picture.

1. Think about the title. What information does it provide? Predict what will be included in the chapter. Change the title to a question that you need to answer as you read.

2. Read the introduction. The details will make more sense if you have an idea of the overall purpose of the reading.

3. Read the summary. Here is where you can get the relationship among the main ideas that were discussed in the introduction.

4. Read the main headings (boldface or italics). These are the main ideas and details that are in the reading.

5. Read the first and last paragraphs of the passage. Once again you will get the main idea of the text.

6. Check the source of the material, the date written, and the author.

Q—**Question**—Questions help the reader focus on ideas and details as they read. Questions become a criterion to use to determine if details are relevant or important.

1. Use the questions at the beginning or end of the text.

2. Formulate questions by changing main headings and subheads into questions. Example: Causes of the Civil War. What were the causes of the Civil War?

3. Formulate questions based on the first sentence of each paragraph.

R—**Read** the text with a purpose to answer the questions that you have made. Move quickly. Sort out ideas and evaluate them. If the content does not relate directly to the questions, move on. The key is to read selectively based on the questions you have developed.

R—**Recite** by making brief notes about the text or by using recitation (discussion) with a partner or in a small group. Think about the answers to your questions and answer the questions in your own words, not the author's. Write answers using only key words, lists, graphic organizers, that will help you recall the whole idea.

R—**Review** what you have learned by rereading your notes and by generating, answering, and discussing the questions. Try to recite the answers to your questions without using your notes.

READING STRATEGY 20—DRTA

Directed Reading Thinking Activity (DRTA) encourages students to become active participants in the reading process. It helps students set purposes for their reading and helps them comprehend text.

The steps are very similar to the KWL strategy:

1. **Pool Information**—Students combine their information and answer the question, "What do we already know about the topic?" This activates their prior knowledge.

2. **Develop Questions**—What do we want to find out about the topic?

3. **Search**—Read to find the answers to our questions.

4. **Analyze**—Which questions were answered? Which questions were not answered?

5. **Look Further**—Search for the answers to questions that were not answered.

JUST FOR FUN—A Flip Book

Flip books are a creative way to take notes, write definitions, formulas, or concepts that you want students to remember and share. Create the book with the number of edges that you need. Each edge will be labeled with a topic, skill, concept, formula, or word that your students need to learn or review. *Students who usually won't take notes will make and use a flip book!*

Step-by-step Directions for Making a Flip Book

1. Take two sheets of paper and fold the two sheets "hot dog" style (the long way). Tear them in half, creating four long, narrow sheets of paper.

2. Place the four sheets of paper in a stack so that the bottoms and tops are even.

3. Slide each of the top three sheets up until the bottom of the four sheets are staggered with an equal space showing on each sheet.

4. Fold the tops of the sheets over so that the staggered edges have the same space showing all the way down the book. The flip book will have eight flaps that can be labeled and "flipped" up for notetaking.

5. Staple the top and you have a flip book!

Final Thoughts About Reading Strategies

Casey Stengel, a famous baseball coach, was talking about coaching a team when he said, "It's easy to get good players—getting them to work together is the hard part." To paraphrase and relate his sentiment to reading: "It's easy to find reading strategies—teaching them to students is the hard part."

Sometimes enthusiastic, well-meaning teachers learn a new reading strategy and expect their students to use it without actually teaching and modeling the strategy. It is important for students to internalize strategies so that they become a part of how they read in all their subjects. So, it is vitally important that teachers explicitly teach the strategies, model the strategies, and then supervise as students practice the strategies.

DID YOU KNOW?

The 80-15-5 Rule: Any one technique works well with 80 percent of students, okay with 15 percent of students, and not at all with 5 percent of students.

CHAPTER 5

TEACHING THE STRATEGIES

"Learn from the mistakes of others—
you can't live long enough to make
them all yourself."

— *Unknown*

The Importance of Explicit Instruction

Teachers generally love their subject areas and have chosen to teach that particular subject. *(Think about how many classes you took in college just to find out more about your favorite subject!)* Not surprisingly, teachers think *their* content is interesting to everyone. Unfortunately, this is not the case. Teachers also think that their particular subject areas are not that difficult to understand, if students would just study and pay attention. These teachers have forgotten the hours they spent in university classes. They have the teachers' guides that go with their current textbook and many of them have taught the same subject for years! For most students, content classes *(including English)* are like foreign languages that have to be suffered through and learned as part of school.

If today's content teachers use text and instructional methods that highlight what is interesting about their subjects and emphasize the content that is relevant to students' lives, they have a much better chance of engaging students positively. Middle school students can find curriculum-based information interesting. There is one problem with this approach to teaching and learning. Today's schools are achievement driven, so middle school teachers must balance what works best to raise test scores with improving reading comprehension and motivating their students to learn. Adding what research has found to be true about older readers' comprehension and motivation problems requires that teachers look carefully at instructional practices and students' literacy needs.

Research verifies that teachers using their specific content to explicitly teach literacy strategies successfully motivate older readers to read and help them improve their comprehension. So once a teacher selects an appropriate reading strategy, that strategy must be explicitly taught.

Effectively teaching a strategy involves a number of steps. This chapter will provide a lesson plan format that makes it easy for content area teachers to:

- Provide explicit instruction in comprehension strategies for their content using metacognitive instruction

- Explain, model, and guide practice until students apply strategies independently, flexibly, and in combination

- Provide instruction before, during, and after reading text

- Promote thinking and elaboration by asking questions, encouraging student questions and discussions, and using a variety of scaffolding techniques for reading new and difficult content

- Prepare for instruction by anticipating specific problems that students will encounter with content area text (prior knowledge/experiences, vocabulary, sentence structures, literary techniques, fluency)

- Use ongoing monitoring to adjust instruction, correct misconceptions, and measure progress

Some Questions to Ask Before Having Students Read

If middle grades teachers want to help their students with reading comprehension, they need to keep the following questions in mind before they teach a lesson:

1. Am I helping students activate or build on prior knowledge?

2. Am I encouraging active involvement by the students? Am I using student-centered *(rather than teacher-directed)* learning?

3. Do my students have time to work together during the learning process?

4. Are there opportunities for students to understand what they are learning (the content), how they are learning it (the process), and why they are learning it (the reason)?

5. Have I helped my students analyze the text structure and how the information is organized?

6. Am I modeling strategies for my students and telling them my thought process and exactly what (and how) I am thinking?

7. Am I giving direct instruction of important vocabulary, concepts, formulas, that allows students to be involved actively?

8. Am I intentionally teaching comprehension strategies to my students until their use becomes automatic?

9. Can I integrate the reading comprehension strategies before, during, and after reading?

Metacognitive Instruction

Metacognition means to "think about what you are thinking." As simple as that may sound, many students don't think about what they are thinking or doing as they interact with text. They think they are reading because their eyes are passing over the words and they are turning pages. An important role for teachers is to help students learn to "think about what they are thinking and doing" as they read. This is called **metacognitive instruction**. Teachers who use metacognitive instruction provide a structuring mechanism to help students use literacy strategies that will help them comprehend when they read. Content teachers themselves must "think about what they do and think when they read their content," and share those thoughts with their students.

Metacognitive instruction of reading comprehension strategies means that teachers provide a structuring mechanism to help students use the required strategies. This type of support helps students choose an appropriate strategy, plan the sequence of steps required in the strategy, and then monitor how they perform on each step. With consistent and regular practice in these techniques, students begin to develop their own metacognitive understandings, and they begin to generalize them across classes and content areas. Over time, even poor readers will be able to plan, organize, and read successfully.

Metacognitive students will automatically:

- use prior knowledge to make new information relevant and more meaningful;

- focus their reading by determining the most important ideas and themes in a text and excluding unimportant information;

- question themselves, the authors, and the texts they read to clarify and focus their reading;

- create visual and sensory images to help understand the text;

- draw conclusions, make judgments and predictions, and interpret new ideas;

- Synthesize and summarize what has been read;

- Utilize a variety of fix-up strategies to repair comprehension when it breaks down.

Scaffolding

The concept of scaffolding learning for students is similar to scaffolding in construction. When builders need to construct a tall building, they use scaffolds to get the workmen to the place they need to be to do the work.

The same thing happens in the classroom. Teachers must begin with what students already know and understand, and then scaffold (or support) the students as they add new concepts. The scaffold provides a framework that moves students from what they know to the new information.

Scaffolding for student learning can come in many forms: verbal assistance, modeling, and particularly graphic organizers. Scaffolding must activate relevant prior knowledge of the content before, during, and after reading text. The goal is for students to use what they already know to help them store newly learned information with other related memories. Typical types of scaffolding techniques are:

- providing hints or clues

- reminding students about previous learning

- providing background information or a reference that can be used

- providing graphic organizers like charts, pictures, labels, maps, grids, graphs, study guides, anticipation guides, chapter maps, or check lists

- underlining or highlighting key words in the instructions

With these techniques in mind, the following is a sample lesson format that can be used when teaching a comprehension strategy. It is a combination of the Madeline Hunter six-point lesson plan and a variety of other plans. *It is common practice for schools to have teachers write and turn in lesson plans, so substitute the appropriate labels for your school if they are different from the ones given here.* Even when using the lesson plan format mandated by a particular school, incorporate the following steps for teaching reading strategies to students until they become automatic. At the end of this chapter, scripted lessons in this format provide classroom examples of scaffolding.

Lesson Format for Teaching a Reading Comprehension Strategy

STEP ONE: Hook the Students

Activate prior knowledge by connecting the new strategy to something students already know or believe. Get them emotionally involved in the lesson. Use humor, a personal story, or create relevance to their lives by telling them that knowing this strategy will help them get better grades, be better readers, historians, scientists, or mathematicians.

The brain seeks novelty, and students have to become engaged or they will not listen. This is a critical step in teaching a lesson because brain research shows that emotion drives attention, attention drives understanding and learning, and understanding and learning drive memory (Jensen, 1998).

If students do not have any prior knowledge about the subject *(which is often true in middle school)*, give them a solid base of background information on which to build new material. Without making these connections, there may not be long-term recall.

STEP TWO: Whole Group Instruction

State the objective for teaching a specific reading strategy. Be very specific about what the strategy is, how the strategy works, and why it is important to know it in the particular subject area. This is the part of the lesson where students receive handouts and the teacher writes on the board or overhead or whatever is normally done when teaching content. This is the teacher input part of the lesson. *Remember to put some life into the presentation to keep the students' attention!*

STEP THREE: *Me (Think Aloud One—Teacher Only)*

Once the content of the lesson has been explained, the teacher models the skill or strategy and explains exactly what he or she is thinking (the process) using a Think Aloud. In this first Think Aloud, do not be tempted to include the students when modeling the strategy. Show them how a good reader in this subject "thinks." Of all the steps, this is the hardest because teachers have always been taught to interact with students and keep them actively engaged. Some students will even try to "help" when their teacher first starts doing this Think Aloud process.

Another reason that this first Think Aloud may be challenging is because it is difficult to explain the thinking process exactly. Many teachers have never analyzed the process themselves, so figure out the steps **before** sharing with students. Most of what the students will learn about the comprehension strategy, they will learn from this teacher demonstration. *What they see their teacher do is what they will try to do themselves.* Therefore, it is essential that the teacher be comfortable with the strategies and comfortable with "thinking aloud."

STEP FOUR: *We (Think Aloud Two—Teacher and Students Together)*

This is the student interaction step where students are engaged and think with the teacher using the Think Aloud strategy. The students have heard the teacher "think through" the process once; now they model the process again, this time with their own involvement.

STEP FIVE: *Two (Guided Practice)*

This step ensures that all the students participate. Use common sense to do what is best in a particular class during this step where the kids work collaboratively in groups of two or three. Remember, this step is guided practice, so the teacher will observe or assist the kids as needed. This is no time to sit at the desk or do "administrivia." Teachers should use this step to assess the students' interactions to determine if they understand how the reading strategy works. If students do not get it, go back to Step Three and reteach before moving on to independent practice.

STEP SIX: *You (Independent Practice)*

If students do not seem to grasp the information at this point, go back again before continuing the lesson. Remember the old saying, "Practice makes perfect."? There's an important addition to that adage—Practicing **correctly** makes perfect.

Brain researchers report, "Practice makes permanent," so make sure students know and understand the reading strategy before they ever start independent practice. Students do not need to practice doing something wrong.

STEP SEVEN: *Closure*

This is the time to review what students have learned about the strategy and discuss how they might use it when they are reading in other classes or taking a test.

Sample Lesson Plans

A few words of caution:

- When you introduce a comprehension strategy, use content that all students can understand easily.

- The topic should not be too interesting; otherwise students focus on what they are reading rather than on how they are reading.

How to Teach Reading . . .

This is critical because the focus of the lesson should be on the strategy itself.

- To teach a new strategy, try using a story or a chapter that has already been read and perhaps even previously assessed. The students will think they already know the content, and they certainly will not find it overly fascinating reading. They will think it is easy to read and then they can focus on the strategy that is being taught instead of the materials.

- When the lesson is finished, students should be able to describe the strategy, explain how to do it, and tell how it relates to the text they read. *They should not be talking about the content of what they just read.*

Customize these plans to fit your content and teaching style.

Sample Lesson Plan 1:
QAR—Question-Answer Relationships

Objective: Student uses the four types of Question-Answer Relationships to locate answers to comprehension questions.

Note: *If absorbing the four QARs together is too difficult for your students, teach QAR in two sessions. The first session should focus only on the two literal QARs, while the second session then focuses on the two inferential QARs. Teachers are sometimes surprised by how difficult it is for students to differentiate between* **Think and Search** *and* **The Author and Me** *questions. That is why it may be necessary to introduce and practice them separately.*

STEP ONE: *Hook the Students*

Sample Teacher Script:

"Have you ever had a teacher ask you to read something for a class, like a story or a chapter, and then you had to answer questions about what you read? Well, of course you have; you're in school and that's what teachers do at school. But what I'd really like to know is: have any of you ever had trouble answering some of the questions and getting the right answers?

Well, this kind of thing happens to everyone, unless you know some tricks that good readers use when they answer questions. For example, sometimes the answer to a question is right there in one sentence of what we are reading, and it even has the same words that are in the question. At other times, we have to come up with an answer for a question by putting together ideas from several sentences that may not even be together in the same paragraph.

Today I'm going to share with you a reading tool or trick that good readers (historians, mathematicians, scientists) use when they have to answer questions about something they have read. It's called Q-A-R, which stands for Question-Answer Relationships."

STEP TWO: *Whole Group Instruction*

This is the part of the lesson where the teacher actually teaches the strategy. Provide students with a written and verbal description of each type of question-answer relationship. Distribute the handout (page 153) with the four types of questions

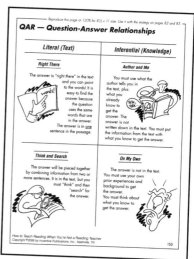

How to Teach Reading . . .

explained. Have each type of question written on card stock and laminated so they can be put on the learning wall as each one is explained. Go over the handouts with the students and discuss the four kinds of questions. Consider using an overhead of the handout to teach from and refer to as each QAR is explained.

STEP THREE: Me (Think Aloud One—Teacher Only)

Sample Teacher Script:

"Today we are going to read a chapter on the parts of plants. Now we read this chapter a few weeks ago, so I know that you all know what it says, and we've already had the test. Most of you did well on that test, too. Well, almost all of you did well.

At any rate, remember that today we're not worried about what the chapter is about because our purpose is to learn how to read a chapter and then be able to identify what kinds of questions we are being asked to answer using Question-Answer relationships. After you learn the QAR strategy, maybe on the next chapter you will be able to answer every question on the test correctly, and everybody will make an A. I think that would be great!

So, the first thing a good reader always does is read the questions at the end of the chapter before he ever starts reading. This way, we'll know exactly what it is that we are reading to learn.

After we read the questions, I'm going to read the first few paragraphs aloud to you, and I want you to follow along with me as I read. After I finish reading the first few paragraphs, I'm going to model for you what I would do, how my brain would be thinking, to answer the questions at the end of the chapter using the four kinds of QAR questions."

STEP FOUR: We (Think Aloud Two—<u>Teacher and Students Together</u>)

Sample Teacher Script:

> "Now that I've shown you how I would use the four kinds of QARs on these first two paragraphs, we're going to read the next two paragraphs together. I'll read aloud and you follow along with me. When we finish reading, we'll practice the questions together and see if you understand how to do QARs."

After reading the passage, ask one question from each QAR category. Point out the differences between each question and the type of answer it requires. You may have to do this several times. After students demonstrate that they understand the differences among the four QAR levels, go to the next part of the lesson.

STEP FIVE: Two (Guided Practice)

Sample Teacher Script:

> "You guys did a great job with those paragraphs, so now you're going to work with a partner and make up four questions, one for each kind of QAR, from the next two paragraphs in the chapter. Just follow these steps":

1. Read the assigned paragraphs with your partner. Remember that each person must read at least one paragraph out loud while the partner follows along.

2. When you finish reading, you will work together and make up four questions—one for each QAR—and write them on your individual papers.

3. For each question you will:

   • Write which type of QAR it is.

- Write where the answer to the question is found in the paragraphs (paragraph and line). You don't have to copy the sentence from the paragraphs.

- Write why (the reasons) the questions represent one QAR but not another.

When everyone is finished, you and your partner will share your questions with another pair of students and see if they can identify your QARs."

After students have done this step, discuss as a class what each group considers their best question for each level of QAR.

STEP SIX: *You (Independent Practice)*

If time permits in class, have students read more of the chapter alone and then write two questions, tell what kind of QAR each one is, tell why the question represents a certain QAR, and tell where the information is in the passage. If the students understand the strategy, assign this for homework.

STEP SEVEN: *Closure*

Sample Teacher Script:

"You guys did great today. Let's quickly review the four kinds of question-answer relationships. Now that you know what it is, what do you think about QAR? Is it something you think will help you in other classes? Explain why (the reasons) you think that. Will it help you when you take tests? Why do you think it will/won't?"

Sample Lesson Plan 2:
Sort Activity for Math Vocabulary

Objective: Students will be able to match math terms and definitions
using a sort activity.

This activity can be used before teaching the chapter as a
pre-assessment of prior knowledge, a reinforcer, or a review.

STEP ONE: Hook the Students

Sample Teacher Script:

"Have you ever noticed how many words are in the math
textbook? Not only do you have to know numbers and math
formulas, but you also have to know math terms. Sometimes
it is very difficult to keep all the formulas and terms straight.
Remember when you were first learning your timetables in
elementary school? I bet one of the things you did to
memorize them was to use flash cards, or maybe you had to
write them over and over. We've covered a lot of material in
this chapter, and some of it is confusing, so today we're
going to use a strategy that many mathematicians use when
they need to remember a lot of important math information.
It is an activity that will help you remember the important
terms and formulas for this chapter. We are going to do a
math sort! It is a way of categorizing or grouping terms and
formulas so we can remember them."

STEP TWO: Whole Group Instruction

In this lesson, use terms with their definitions. Reproduce the math terms
on pages 160–162. Use one color of paper for the terms and another
color for the definitions. Make enough sets for students to work in pairs
with a few extra just in case. As usual, laminate the sheets before they are

cut up. Use different example terms when modeling than the ones the students will use to do the sort in step three.

Sample Teacher Script:

> "I bet you've sorted lots of things before. Anybody have to do their own laundry at home? Do you put all the clothes together when you wash them, or do you sort them into groups by colors? Well, a sorting activity is exactly the same idea. I have a baggie with terms, formulas, and definitions in it. The purpose of this kind of sort is to match the terms or formulas with their definitions. First, I'm going to show you how I would do a sort like this."

STEP THREE: *Me (Think Aloud One—Teacher Only)*

Sample Teacher Script:

> "I bet you're thinking 'Why does she need to show us how to do this? After all, how hard can it be to dump out some terms and definitions and match them up?' Well, that's exactly why I'm going to show you how a mathematician would do this sort. There is thinking involved! O.K., I get my baggie and notice that there are two different colors of paper in it. Hmmm. I wonder if that's important or means anything. I guess I'll take a look and see. Oh, I see—the terms and formulas are one color and the definitions are another. That's good to know and that should help me. I think I'll start with the ones I know and then go to the hard ones. In fact, I think I'll make three stacks as I take out the terms or formulas. I'm going to put the ones I know for sure in one stack, the ones I think I know in another, and the ones I'm clueless about in a third stack. This way I can work quickly when I take out the definitions. I'll be able to match them up easily with the ones I know and then guess with the ones that are left over."

As you talk this through, use the samples from your baggie. Make sure to have a few extra to do with the students in the next think aloud.

STEP FOUR: *We (Think Aloud Two—<u>Teacher and Students Together</u>)*

Sample Teacher Script:

> "Now that I've shown you how I would do this activity, let's match a few together."

STEP FIVE: *Two (Guided Practice)*

Sample Teacher Script:

> "O.K. you are ready to work together. I've got a baggie for each pair, but don't open your baggie until everyone gets theirs. I want you all to start together and see which team finishes first. Ready, go."

STEP SIX: *You (Independent Practice)*

Sample Teacher Script:

> "Now that you know how a sort works for remembering math terms, I want you to think of three words that I didn't include in my sort. Think of three words that you think are important and put them on these index cards. Write the term on one index card and put the definition on another. When everyone finishes, you'll share them with your partner and see if your partner knows them."

STEP SEVEN: *Closure*

Sample Teacher Script:

> "Good job today. Do you think doing sorts will help you remember math terms from now on? Is this a good way to review for a test? We're going to make up some new sorts using the words each of you came up with today, and use sorts again when we have time."

Sample Lesson Plan 3:
Chapter Mapping

Objective: The students will be able to map a section of the text before reading to identify important information.

This lesson can be used with any textbook in any class. Students often struggle to make sense of their textbook readings, so this pre-reading strategy helps develop direction and background so they can better learn what is important in their reading.

Buehl calls this a "frontloading technique" to guide readers through a chapter and to point out features of the text that warrant close attention. Students will answer the question, "What can readers do to understand the text features of this specific textbook before reading?"

STEP ONE: Hook the Students

Sample Teacher Script:

"Have you ever had to read a chapter or a story and then answer questions or work problems about what you read? Well, of course you have. Teachers do that all the time in school. Have you ever noticed that a lot of the information in the chapter or story was not part of the information you needed to know to answer the questions? A lot of the information you read was extra information that was not important.

The key for good readers is to be able to look at all of the information presented and figure out what is important to remember and what is not important to know. This is a skill that takes practice. Most textbooks have far more information in them than you need to remember, so today, I'm going to show you a reading strategy called chapter mapping. Sometimes this reading strategy is called a chapter tour because the reader becomes a guide and takes a tour of the chapter before reading it.

Chapter mapping will help you decide before you ever read the chapter, what things will be important to remember and which things you can skim over quickly. You can do a survey of the chapter and find out what to look for when you read. The idea is that before you spend lots of time reading every single thing in the chapter, you figure out in advance what is important. This approach will save you time and allow you to cover more information quickly. You'll also have notes to study by when it comes time to take a test."

STEP TWO: *Whole Group Instruction*

This is the part of the lesson where the teacher directly and explicitly teaches the steps in the strategy. Be very specific about what the strategy is, how the strategy works, and why it is important to know it in your content area. Consider using an overhead or a power point slide to teach from and to refer to as you explain the strategy. Another option is to have students do a foldable to keep their notes on as they select important information. *(Remember, the power of visualization helps commit information to long-term memory!)*

Sample Teacher Script:

"Here is a study guide that tells you the parts of a chapter map, and then the things you must look for in each textbook, because each one is different. You need to think about a lot of things before you ever start to read, so you won't waste time and energy trying to remember information that is not important." *[Go over the Chapter Map Study Guide of the seven things to think about when previewing a text—page 163.]*

"Now that we know how we're going to preview or map the chapter, let's make a flip book (or foldable) to keep our notes in order. We're going to make a flip book with seven tabs, one for each of the important things we must think about before we read. If we do a good job of previewing the chapter before we read it, this graphic organizer can become our notes for the chapter and can be used as a study guide for the test.

Before you read a chapter, preview what is in the chapter. Create a mental map to follow, because each subject's textbook is written in a special way to emphasize that subject. You must look at how each textbook is written to understand the major ideas that need to be remembered."

STEP THREE: *Me (Think Aloud One—<u>Teacher Only</u>)*

Sample Teacher Script:

"Doing a chapter map is like doing what a quarterback would do in a football game. Before he runs a play, he takes the time at the line of scrimmage to look carefully at the defense players. He wants to know what to expect and wants to make predictions of what might happen. He wants to anticipate or think about in advance the strategies he'll need to use to make his play call successful. That's exactly what a good reader does before you read a large amount of information. You preview the material to figure out what your strategies for success are going to be. Let's turn in our books to the new chapter on page ____. I'm going to follow the seven steps we just talked about in previewing the chapter, and show you how I would think through these seven things before I begin to read. I'm going to think ahead just like a quarterback has to do in a game."

(Use the overhead and lead the students through the seven ideas. Make sure you tell them what you are thinking about the seven things and why they are important for your content.)

STEP FOUR: *We (Think Aloud Two: <u>Teacher and Students Together</u>)*

Sample Teacher Script:

"Now that I've shown you how I would think about the chapter in seven steps before I begin reading, let's look together at the Specific Text Features and see how they apply to our book."

Use the Specific Text Features Checklist (page 164) and begin going through the five text feature points. Include the students and let them help, but continue to model what you are thinking as you write your notes and they do the same thing on their sheets. Remember to point out things that are specific to your content that may not be true in all textbooks.

STEP FIVE: *TWO (Guided Practice)*

Sample Teacher Script:

"Now that we have done the preview of this chapter together and started our chapter map flip book, I want you to work with a partner and look at the next chapter. I know we haven't studied it yet either, but remember I'm trying to teach you a reading strategy that you use before you read a chapter. I want you to see if the next chapter is set up like

the one we just did together. Is our textbook predictable about how we can figure out what is important information? If it is, this will mean we can always see what we need to know for the test before we ever start reading. Hopefully, this will save you a lot of time and energy!

Draw a line under what we just wrote about this chapter OR make another flip book so you and your partner can map chapter ___ together. Follow the study guide like we did together, and talk about what you discover about how our textbook works."

STEP SIX: *YOU (Independent Practice)*

For homework have students use their study guide sheet and map a section of the chapter we are currently studying to see if the text follows the same format for all the chapters.

STEP SEVEN: *Closure*

Sample Teacher Script:

"Good job today. Now that you know what it means to preview a chapter and do a chapter map before you read the chapter, do you think you can use them in other classes when you have to read? What makes you think that? Will chapter maps help you when you take tests? What makes you think that?"

Sample Lesson Plan 4:
Paired Reading and Questioning

Objective: The students will be able to collaboratively read a
passage and comprehend vocabulary and main
ideas or concepts.

The purpose of this lesson is to teach the literacy
strategy of Paired Reading and Questioning. Students are
often asked to read paragraphs, chapters, or word
problems that have vocabulary and content that are
unfamiliar to them. In an effort to decode the words or
symbols and understand the new content at the same time,
students cannot read and understand what they are
reading. When students are told to read the material silently
or teachers call on individuals to read for the class, the
same problem occurs. Paired Reading and Questioning is
an effective strategy that requires collaborative learning to
help all students better learn the content and read for
comprehension. It can be used in all content areas.
Reproduce pages 165 and 166 to be used in the lesson.

STEP ONE: *Hook the Students*

Sample Teacher Script:

> "Have you ever had a teacher ask you to read
> something for a class, like a story or a chapter,
> but as you read and figure out the new words,
> you have a hard time understanding what you are
> reading? Well, this kind of thing happens to
> everyone unless you know some tricks that good

readers use when they read new material. One thing good readers often do is to read new material out loud so they can hear the new words or ideas first. Then they go back and read the material again to figure out what it means. Today, I'm going to share with you a reading tool or trick called Paired Reading and Questioning where you practice with a partner how to read new material and figure out what it means."

STEP TWO: *Whole Group Instruction*

Sample Teacher Script:

"Here is the direction sheet for the reading strategy called Paired Reading and Questioning *(page 165).* I'm also giving you the sheet *(page 166)* that you'll use to write the important points you'll find in the reading as we practice the strategy."

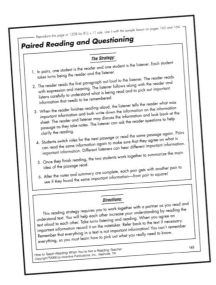

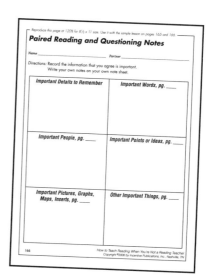

STEP THREE: *Me (Think Aloud One—<u>Teacher Only</u>)*

Sample Teacher Script:

> **"Now that you know what we're going to do, I want** (*pick a student or ask for a volunteer*) **to help me show you how to do Paired Reading and Questioning when you get with your partner. This is what it should look like and what I want to see when you work with your partner."**

> *Reverse roles with the student and model both parts—Reader and Listener—so students can see exactly how the teacher would do each one.*

STEP FOUR: *We (Think Aloud Two: <u>Teacher and Students Together</u>)*

For this strategy, Think Aloud Two is the teacher's option. If you think it necessary, you can ask two students to model what you have just done in Think Aloud One. It often takes more than one modeling for students to understand the task. Make sure as the students work together that you watch carefully. They should be doing exactly what you did when you modeled in Think Aloud One.

Have the pair read to each other the next paragraph, and when they finish their roles, stop and make specific comments about behaviors that you liked that you observed in the pair—the listener followed along with the reader and concentrated on what was being read instead of writing during the reading; the reader reads with expression and meaning so the listener could understand, the two worked together to write the notes and discussed what was important; the two looked back at the passage to verify what was important.

You want all the students to know what is best and what you like

How to Teach Reading . . .

to see happening. If you don't think an additional demonstration is needed, move on to Step Five, which is guided practice.

Sample Teacher Script:

> **"Now that I've shown you what Paired Reading and Questioning should look like, I'd like for two of you to do the next paragraph for the class. The class is going to watch, and we'll see how it goes and offer our comments. Who thinks you understand Paired Reading and Questioning and would like to demonstrate the strategy for us?"**

STEP FIVE: *TWO (Guided Practice)*

Sample Teacher Script:

> **"You guys did a great job showing us how to do Paired Reading and Questioning, so now everyone will do the next paragraph with your partner. Remember all the things we've talked about and really try to do them as you are the reader or the listener."**

STEP SIX: *YOU (Independent Practice)*

If time permits, have pairs work independently on the next paragraphs while you walk around the room and observe.

STEP SEVEN: *Closure*

Have students discuss how this reading strategy might help them as they read new information.

Sample Teacher Script:

> "Good job today. Paired Reading and Questioning is a reading strategy that good readers use to help them learn new material. Do you think it helped you today to gather the important information from what we read? Was it easier to work with a partner and concentrate on either reading or listening? Is it something you think will help you in other classes? What makes you think that? Will it help you when you take tests? What makes you think that?"

Final Thoughts on Teaching Reading Comprehension Strategies

Reading to learn content is an interactive process used before reading, during reading, and after reading. In order for students to engage actively in reading the content of their subjects, which often contains new information and subject-specific language, is difficult to understand, and not written in an exciting way, teachers must use the reading comprehension strategies that are most effective in their subject areas. Use the following guidelines to choose the strategies appropriate for a particular classroom:

- Select strategies that are used by readers of the subject in real life.

- Comprehension strategies should be taught over time during the year.

- Teach one strategy at a time.

- Strategies need to be explicitly taught in the context of reading the content.

- Each new strategy needs to be modeled and explained.

- Supported, structured practice of each strategy needs to be provided (scaffolding).

- Plenty of practice is provided for each strategy.

- Students need to learn that reading is highly personal because it is a reflective and intentional process.

- Comprehension strategies need to be taught and used throughout the school day in all content areas to show how they are effective with any subject.

Remember, content teachers need to teach strategies that get students to think not only about what they are going to read, but also about how they will read it.

"If you can imagine a thing, conjure it up in space, then you can make it . . . The universe is real but you can't see it. You have to imagine it. Then you can be realistic about reproducing it."

— *Alexander Calder, sculptor*

CHAPTER 6

CONCLUSION

"We can't keep teaching the same old ways, cause if
we keep on doing what we've always been doing,
we'll keep on getting what we've always been getting."

— *Unknown*

Understanding the Learning Process

In his book *Powerful Learning*, Ron Brandt summarized the learning process with the following statements:

1. People learn what is personally meaningful to them.

2. People learn when they accept challenging but achievable goals.

3. Learning is developmental.

4. Individuals learn differently.

5. People construct new knowledge by building on their current knowledge.

6. Much learning occurs through social interaction.

7. People need feedback to learn.

8. Successful learning involves the use of strategies—which themselves must be learned.

9. A positive emotional climate strengthens learning.

10. Learning is influenced by total environment.

These ten statements not only summarize the learning process, but also clarify what this book has been saying about teaching reading. In order for middle grades students to become successful readers across the curriculum, every teacher must become not only a teacher of their own subject area, but also a teacher of reading comprehension strategies. Since good readers use a variety of strategies to make sense out of what

CHAPTER 6

they are reading, it is the teachers' responsibility to help students be aware of the strategies that work best with their content. The strategies taught need to be flexible and adaptable to meet the needs of any reading problem.

Ask the Questions

These critical questions must be addressed by content area teachers as they become teachers of reading strategies:

1. **What do good readers in my content area do as they read?**
   Find out this information and model it.

2. **How can I create a supportive context for comprehension development in my classroom?**
   A supportive environment assures students that they really can learn to read the text in a particular subject.

3. **How can I design and implement activities that will support reading comprehension?**
   Which format or lesson plan will I use?
   This is the model of what you plan to do, and it will force you to plan to intentionally and explicitly include reading strategies in your lessons.

4. **Which comprehension strategies will I teach? When will I teach them? How will I teach them? How will I provide explicit instruction in the use of reading comprehension strategies for my students?**
   You know your subject area scope and sequence, so now decide how to use your content as a vehicle to also teach reading strategies.

134

Create a Personal Action Plan

Now that you have read *How to Teach Reading When You're Not a Reading Teacher*, you are ready to develop a personal action plan. Use the action plan form on page 167. Take the time to think it through and fill it out. Address the four critical areas that will help you teach reading in your classroom.

Success always begins with a plan. When your plan is complete, sign and date your commitment. During the year, try to teach your students at least one comprehension strategy each grading period.

You are beginning a very rewarding phase in your teaching career. You are no longer just an English, math, science, or social studies teacher. Instead, you are now an English, math, science, or social studies teacher who teaches reading!

Reproduce this page at 120% for 8½ x 11 size. Use it with page 135

My Personal Action Plan

My Goal: What do good readers in my subject do when they read?

_____

_____

The Environment: How can I change my classroom setting or routine to help me teach my students to read better? How can I create a supportive environment?

_____

_____

The Model: How can I design and implement activities that will help reading comprehension? What format or lesson plan will I use?

_____

_____

The Curriculum: Which strategies will I teach? When will I teach them? How will I teach them?

_____

_____

Signature _____ **Date** _____

How to Teach Reading When You're Not a Reading Teacher
Copyright ©2006 by Incentive Publications, Inc. Nashville, TN

167

APPENDIX

Good Reader Bookmark

GOOD READER BOOKMARK

Before I read
I ask myself these questions:

- What do I need to know before I read this material?

- What do I already know about the topic?

- How is the text organized to help me?

- What is the reason I am reading this material?

- What is the author's reason for writing this material?

- Am I reading for my own pleasure? If so, I can read at whatever pace I choose.

- Am I reading for school? If so, I have to ask some different kinds of questions as I read.

- Does the title tell me what the reading is about?

- Are there pictures, graphs, maps, titles, headings, boldface, or italics that can help me?

- Can I create a graphic organizer that will help me organize what I am going to read in a way that I can understand?

GOOD READER BOOKMARK

While I read
I ask myself these questions:

- How does this connect to what I know?
- How does what I am reading compare to what I thought I knew?
- Does what I am reading make sense? If it does not, what is it that I don't understand?
- Do I need to code the text and note what is important, what I don't understand, what I need to reread?
- Do I need to mark important words or ideas with highlighting, underlining, or sticky notes?
- Do I need to go back and reread all or part of the material?
- Do the pictures, charts, graphs, or other visual aids help me understand what I am reading or give me more information that I need to know?
- Do I agree with the way the problem was solved? Am I surprised about the information? Is the information believable? Have I seen or heard something like this before?
- Are there clues for me so I can predict what the story is about and the problems that the characters will face? What descriptions do I need to remember?
- What is the plot or theme?
- What mental pictures do I see?
- What connections can I make from this passage to others that we have read in class?
- Who or what is the story about?
- When and where does the story take place?
- How and why do the events happen?
- Is there a specific problem that is solved?
- Do I see words that I don't know?

GOOD READER BOOKMARK

After I read
I ask myself these questions:

- Did I find the answers to the questions I needed to answer?

- Did I learn what I wanted to learn?

- Were there other questions that I found?

- Were there questions or problems I didn't find?

- What do I know now that I did not know before?

- What is the most surprising or interesting thing I read?

- What new terms, concepts, or vocabulary did I learn?

- What do I remember?

- How do I feel about what I have read?

- Does my graphic organizer (if any) make sense?

- Can I restate the main points in my own words?

- How can I apply what I just read to my schoolwork and my life?

- Is there a lesson or moral in the story?

Wordo Grid

		FREE		

KWL Chart

K *What* *I Know*	W *What I* *Want to Know*	L *What I* *Learned*
BEFORE READING	**BEFORE READING**	**AFTER READING**
Put what you know here	*Write two or three questions* *you have here*	*Write answers to your questions* *and important information here*

KWWL Chart

K *What I Know*	**W** *What I Want to Know*	**W** *Where I can find the information*	**L** *What I Learned*
BEFORE READING	**BEFORE READING**	**DURING READING**	**AFTER READING**
Put what you know here	*Write two or three questions you have here*	*Tell <u>WHERE</u> you'll look to find your answers*	*Write answers to your questions and important information here*

KWHL Chart

K What I Know	W What I Want to Know	H How I can find the information	L What I Learned
BEFORE READING	**BEFORE READING**	**DURING READING**	**AFTER READING**
Put what you know here	*Write two or three questions you have here*	*Tell HOW you'll find the answers*	*Write answers to your questions and important information here*

How to Teach Reading When You're Not a Reading Teacher

KWGL Chart

K *What* *I Know*	**W** *What I* *Want to Know*	**G** *Where to Go to find* *the information*	**L** *What I* *Learned*
BEFORE READING	**BEFORE READING**	**DURING READING**	**AFTER READING**
Put what you know here	*Write two or three questions you have here*	*Tell where you'll <u>GO</u> to find the answers*	*Write answers to your questions and important information here*

Anticipation Guide

1. _____

   _____

   Notes:

   | **Before Reading** |
   | ○   ○ |
   | Agree   Disagree |
   | **After Reading** |
   | ○   ○ |
   | Agree   Disagree |

2. _____

   _____

   Notes:

   | **Before Reading** |
   | ○   ○ |
   | Agree   Disagree |
   | **After Reading** |
   | ○   ○ |
   | Agree   Disagree |

3. _____

   _____

   Notes:

   | **Before Reading** |
   | ○   ○ |
   | Agree   Disagree |
   | **After Reading** |
   | ○   ○ |
   | Agree   Disagree |

4. _____

   _____

   Notes:

   | **Before Reading** |
   | ○   ○ |
   | Agree   Disagree |
   | **After Reading** |
   | ○   ○ |
   | Agree   Disagree |

5. _____

   _____

   Notes:

   | **Before Reading** |
   | ○   ○ |
   | Agree   Disagree |
   | **After Reading** |
   | ○   ○ |
   | Agree   Disagree |

PIC Form

P	I	C
Put your <u>PURPOSE</u> for reading here	Write three or four <u>IMPORTANT IDEAS,</u> words, or concepts here	Write how what you already knew about the subject <u>CONNECTED</u> with what you learned

PIC Form

P	I	C
Put your <u>PURPOSE</u> for reading here	Write three or four <u>IMPORTANT IDEAS,</u> words, or concepts here	Write how what you already knew about the subject <u>CONNECTED</u> with what you learned

3-2-1

Name _____

3 •

•

•

2 •

•

1

3-2-1

Name _____

3 •

•

•

2 •

•

1

RAFT Planning Sheet

Name _____

Role of the Writer	*Who are you as the writer? A famous person? A character from the reading? A concerned citizen? A reporter?*	
Audience	*Think about your audience. To whom are you writing? Is your audience a friend? Your teacher? Readers of a newspaper?*	
Format	*Consider your purpose, then choose a format. Will your writing persuade, entertain, describe, or inform? What form will the writing take? Is it a letter? A speech? A classified ad? A poem? A help column? A persuasive essay?*	
Topic	*What is your topic? Write a good topic sentence here.*	

Character Wheel Graphic Organizer

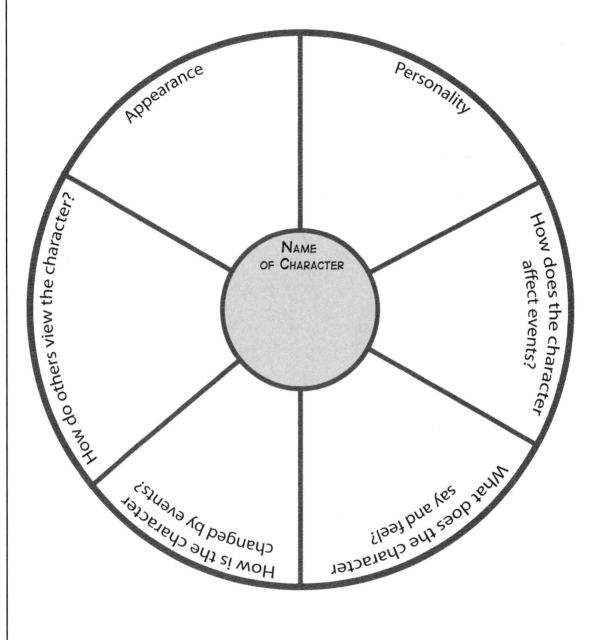

NAME_____

Nonfiction Reading Pyramid Graphic Organizer

TITLE_____

AUTHOR_____

AUDIENCE

PURPOSE

MAIN IDEA

SUPPORTING DETAILS

MAIN IDEA

SUPPORTING DETAILS

MY REACTION

NAME_____

Short Story Graphic Organizer

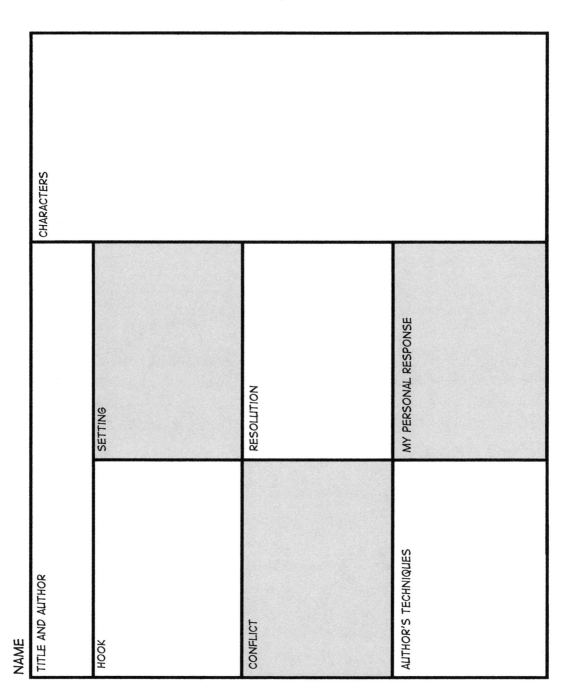

NAME

TITLE AND AUTHOR

CHARACTERS

SETTING

HOOK

RESOLUTION

CONFLICT

MY PERSONAL RESPONSE

AUTHOR'S TECHNIQUES

Column Notes—Two-Column

COLUMN ONE	COLUMN TWO

Column Notes—Three-Column

COLUMN ONE	COLUMN TWO	COLUMN THREE

QAR — *Question-Answer Relationships*

Literal (Text)

Right There

The answer is "right there" in the text, and you can point to the words! It is easy to find the answer because the question uses the same words that are in the answer. The answer is in <u>one</u> sentence in the passage.

Think and Search

The answer will be pieced together by combining information from two or more sentences. It is in the text, but you must "think" and then "search" for the answer.

Inferential (Knowledge)

Author and Me

You must use what the author tells you in the text, plus what you already know to get the answer. The answer is not written down in the text. You must put the information from the text with what you know to get the answer.

On My Own

The answer is not in the text. You must use your own prior experiences and background to get the answer. You must think about what you know to get the answer.

Visual Reading Guides

TOPIC, CHAPTER, OR SECTION

PICTURES		MAPS		MAPS		INSERTS	
Page #	Important information about visual	Page #	Important information about maps	Page #	Important information about maps	Page #	Important information about inserts

Visual Reading Guides

TOPIC, CHAPTER, OR SECTION

Type of visual	Page #	Important information about visual

How to Teach Reading When You're Not a Reading Teacher

RIDER Bookmark

R READ the sentence.

I IMAGINE a picture of it in your mind.

D DESCRIBE how the new image differs from the old.

E EVALUATE to see that the image contains everything.

R REPEAT as you read the next sentence.

AIDE Bookmark

A ACTION—Look for the action in the picture.

I IDEA—Guess the main idea of the picture.

D DETAILS—Study each picture detail.

E EXPLANATION—Read the explanation with the picture.

Reciprocal Teaching

Summarizes

Questions

Clarifies

Predicts

ABC Brainstorming

A	B	C
D	E	F
G	H	I
J	K	L
M	N	O
P	Q	R
S	T	U
V	W	X Y Z

SCAMPER

S
Substitute

C
Combine

A
Adapt

M
Modify

P
Put to other uses

E
Eliminate

R
Reverse or Rearrange

Math Sort

MONOMIAL	**Product of numbers and variables**
BINOMIAL	**Sum or difference of 2 monomials**
TRINOMIAL	**Sum or difference of 3 monomials**
PRIME NUMBER	**A number with exactly 2 factors ("1" and itself)**
RATIO	**Two numbers, division, comparison, colon**
SIMILAR	**Same shape, different size**

Math Sort

COMPLEMENTARY ANGLES	**Sum of measures is 90 degrees**
SUPPLEMENTARY ANGLES	**Sum of measures is 180 degrees**
PYTHAGOREAN THEOREM	**Variables, triangle, right angle, hypotenuse, squared numbers, named after someone**
TRANSLATION	**Slide—requires: direction and number of units**
ROTATION	**Turn—requires: points of rotation, direction, and angles of rotation**
REFLECTION	**Flip—requires: line of reflection**

Math Sort

MEAN	**Average**
MODE	**Data item that appears the most**
FACTOR	**Write a multiplication problem for which you have the answer**
MEDIAN	**Middle number of arranged data**
PROBABILITY	**# of favorable outcomes / # of possible outcomes**

Chapter Map Study Guide

Chapter Map Study Guide

Name

Title
What is the chapter about? What do I already know about this topic? What do I predict I'll know after I read this chapter?

Main Idea
How can I tell what are the most important points in this chapter? How are these points important to me? Why did the author write this? What points should I focus on as I read?

Major Themes
What are the key ideas, concepts, arguments, or conclusions? What are the major points that connect all the details? What does the author believe?

Text Structure
How is the material put together? How is it divided? What part should I focus on?

Important Details
What facts, theories, or formulas are most important? What stands out in the material? Is there text in bold or italic type, quotations, capital letters, different colors? Are there key words or phrases that seem important? How familiar is this material? What details do I already know?

Style
What do I notice about the writing? Are the sentences long and hard to read? Is the vocabulary new or very content specific? How easy will this be to read?

Tone/Attitude/Mood
Does the author have an attitude toward this material? Can I detect any emotion or tone like anger, humor, enthusiasm, criticism, sarcasm, irony, reasoning, persuasion, inspiration, explanation? If the author were to do a live presentation of the material, what would it be like?

Specific Text Features Checklist

☐ 1. The chapter title, any introductory terms or names, the first paragraph of the section—look at the color of the title and sub-titles, are there boxes around information? Is there a time line? Are there focus questions? How is the beginning of the chapter set up to tell you what is important?

☐ 2. Is there a list of objectives, key terms, review questions, essential points, or primary sources? Where are they placed and how do you recognize them?

☐ 3. Look at the opening paragraph of the chapter and of each section. Do they give you the key ideas?

☐ 4. Look at the last paragraph of the chapter and of each section. Do they summarize the key ideas? Do they repeat what was in the opening paragraphs in different words? What is in the review section at the end of the chapter or section?

☐ 5. Look through the chapter and sections for names, dates, words, formulas, or terms that are in bold type, colored print, italics, or that are repeated in more than one place. Are there photographs, charts, maps, bulleted lists, or pictures? Read the captions. Does this give you new information or does it repeat what you've already found?

☐ 1. The chapter title, any introductory terms or names, the first paragraph of the section—look at the color of the title and sub-titles, are there boxes around information? Is there a time line? Are there focus questions? How is the beginning of the chapter set up to tell you what is important?

☐ 2. Is there a list of objectives, key terms, review questions, essential points, or primary sources? Where are they placed and how do you recognize them?

☐ 3. Look at the opening paragraph of the chapter and of each section. Do they give you the key ideas?

☐ 4. Look at the last paragraph of the chapter and of each section. Do they summarize the key ideas? Do they repeat what was in the opening paragraphs in different words? What is in the review section at the end of the chapter or section?

☐ 5. Look through the chapter and sections for names, dates, words, formulas, or terms that are in bold type, colored print, italics, or that are repeated in more than one place. Are there photographs, charts, maps, bulleted lists, or pictures? Read the captions. Does this give you new information or does it repeat what you've already found?

Paired Reading and Questioning

The Strategy:

1. In pairs, one student is the reader, and one student is the listener. Each student takes turns being the reader and the listener.

2. The reader reads the first paragraph out loud to the listener. The reader reads with expression and meaning. The listener follows along with the reader and listens carefully to understand what is being read and to pick out important information that needs to be remembered.

3. When the reader finishes reading aloud, the listener tells the reader what was important information, and both write down the information on the information sheet. The reader and listener may discuss the information and look back at the passage as they take notes. The listener can ask the reader questions to help clarify the reading.

4. Students switch roles for the next passage or read the same passage again. Pairs can read the same information again to make sure that they agree on what is important information. Different listeners can hear different important information.

5. Once they finish reading, the two students work together to summarize the main idea of the passage read.

6. After the notes and summary are complete, each pair gets with another pair to see if they found the same important information—*from pair to square!*

Directions:

This reading strategy requires you to work together with a partner as you read and understand text. You will help each other increase your understanding by reading the text aloud to each other. Take turns listening and reading. When you agree on important information, record it on the notetaker. Refer back to the text if necessary. Remember that not everything in a text is important information! You can't remember everything, so you must learn how to pick out what you really need to know.

Paired Reading and Questioning Notes

Name _____   *Partner* _____

Directions: Record the information that you agree is important.
Write your own notes on your own note sheet.

Important Details to Remember	*Important Words, pg. ____*
Important People, pg. ____	*Important Points or Ideas, pg. ____*
Important Pictures, Graphs, Maps, Inserts, pg. ____	*Other Important Things, pg. ____*

My Personal Action Plan

My Goal: What do good readers in my subject do when they read?

_____

_____

_____

The Environment: How can I change my classroom setting or routine to help me teach my students to read better? How can I create a supportive environment?

_____

_____

_____

The Model: How can I design and implement activities that will help reading comprehension? What format or lesson plan will I use?

_____

_____

_____

The Curriculum: Which strategies will I teach? When will I teach them? How will I teach them?

_____

_____

_____

Signature _____ **Date**_____

GLOSSARY

Affix—a prefix or suffix added to a base word or a root word

Base word—an actual word to which prefixes and/or suffixes may be added

Blue Birds—the large group of students in the middle of the class who come to school because they have to, but perform just enough behaviorally and academically to keep teachers from bothering them. This is the group that can turn into red birds or could become jailbirds depending on teachers' expectations.

Comprehension—understanding, remembering, and communicating with others about what has been read

Comprehension strategies—a set of steps that purposeful, active readers use to make sense of text when they read

Could Become Jailbirds—these are the struggling readers who are academically and behaviorally at risk. If a good teacher does not help these students to become successful in school, they may become another statistic in overcrowded prisons.

Decoding—the process of converting letter symbols and patterns into spoken language

Explicit instruction—a teacher-directed lesson with emphasis on the specific steps needed to master the skill, content, or concept

Expository text—non-fiction or informational text that has specific text features like headings, captions, graphs, charts, tables, diagrams, table of contents, glossary, etc.

Fiction—literature that contains imaginary characters and events; untrue text

Fluency—ability to read text with accuracy, speed, expression, and comprehension; provides the bridge between word recognition and comprehension

Homophones—two or more words that sound alike but have different meanings and spellings. their/there/they're

Homographs—two or more words that are spelled alike but have different meanings and sounds. The homograph must be read in the context of the sentence to determine the pronunciation and meaning. wound/wound, read/read

Inference—a conclusion made by connecting prior knowledge or known information with new information when the meaning isn't obvious in the text; sometimes referred to as "reading between the lines"

Main idea—the central thought or meaning of a piece of text; key things the author wants you to know about the topic; may be stated or implied

Metacognition—"thinking about thinking"—awareness and knowledge of one's mental processes so that one can monitor, regulate, and direct them to a desired end

Morpheme—the smallest unit of meaning in a word; may be a word root like struct, a root word like hand, or an affix like *un-* or *-able*

Narrative text—a text written with a story line; may be fiction or factual events written in the style of a story

Nonfiction text—informational text based upon facts and reality, including textbooks, biography, and reference works

Orthography—the correct sequence of letters in the writing system of a language; correct spelling of a word in the language

Phoneme—the smallest unit of sound in a word, such as the /b/ in the word *bat*

Phonemic Awareness—the ability to hear, identify, and manipulate the individual sounds (phonemes) in spoken words; the awareness is the understanding that the sounds of spoken language work together to make words

Phonics—the understanding that there is a predictable relationship between phonemes (the sounds of a spoken language) and graphemes (the letters) that spell words

Prefix—a letter or letters that carry meaning and are attached to the beginning of a root word or a word root

Read-alouds—text or books read orally for a specific purpose such as to introduce a literary device, an author, a genre, etc. A read aloud model is used to develop students' listening vocabularies, fluency, and general knowledge.

Reading comprehension skills—specific reading skills used to construct meaning from the text. Summarizing, predicting, clarifying and questioning are four of the major comprehension skills.

Red Birds—students who are reading-ready and who come to class understanding the rules of school. They know what to do to make teachers like them and to be academically successful.

Scaffolding instruction—the active monitoring of student learning to add support and guidance through a variety of techniques so a student can successfully make connections between prior knowledge/experience and new information

Semantics—the study of meaning in language; analyzing the meanings of words, phrases, and sentences

Semantic map—graphic organizer that provides a visual display of the relationships between a central concept and a number of ideas that are related to it

Signal words—key words or phrases in text that indicate an organizational or purpose pattern

Sorts—an activity where words, phrases, and concepts are categorized according to specific guidelines

Suffix—a letter or letters that carry meaning and are attached to the end of a base word or root word

Syntax—the structure of language or the rules that govern how words work together in phrases, clauses, and sentences

Systematic instruction—lessons that are planned to meet learners' needs according to a sequence of skills

Visualization—the process of creating mental images from spoken or read words to enhance the comprehension of main ideas and details

Walls that Teach/Word Walls—charts, words, lists or other types of information posted in the classroom for students to use as visual references to enhance long-term memory

Word roots—a Greek or Latin morpheme which usually does not stand alone as a word and to which affixes are attached to form words

Zone of proximal development—Vygotsky's term for the point at which students can be successful with a little help from the teacher; synonyms are instructional level and learning zone

BIBLIOGRAPHY

Allen, Janet. *It's Never Too Late: Leading Adolescents to Lifelong Literacy.* Portsmouth, NH: Heinemann, 1995.

Allen, Janet. *Words, Words, Words: Teaching Vocabulary in Grades 4–12.* Portland, ME: Stenhouse Publishers, 1999.

Barton, M.L. "Addressing the Literacy Crisis: Teaching Reading in the Content Areas," *NASSP Bulletin* 81:587 (1997), 22–30.

Beers, Kylene. *When Kids Can't Read: What Teachers Can Do.* Portsmouth, NH: Heinemann, 2003.

Biancarosa, G., and C.E. Snow. *Reading Next—A Vision for Action and Research in Middle and High School Literacy: A Report to Carnegie Corporation of New York.* Washington, DC: Alliance for Excellent Education, 2004.

Blevins, Wiley. *Building Fluency: Lessons & Strategies for Reading Success.* Jefferson City, MO: Scholastic Professional Books, 2001.

Blevins, Wiley. *Teaching Phonics & Word Study in the Intermediate Grades.* Jefferson City, MO: Scholastic Professional Books, 2001.

Brandt, Ron. *Powerful Learning.* Alexandria, VA: Association for Supervision & Curriculum Development, 1998.

Buehl, Doug. *Classroom Strategies for Interactive Learning,* 2d Ed. Newark, DE: International Reading Association, 2001.

Burns, M. Susan, Peg Griffin, and Catherine Snow, eds. *Starting Out Right: A Guide to Promoting Children's Reading Success.* Washington DC: National Academy Press, 1999.

Cochran, Judith. *As Reading Programs Come and Go This Is What You Need to Know*. Nashville: Incentive Publications, 2002.

Covey, Stephen. *The Seven Habits of Highly Effective People*. New York: Simon & Schuster, 1989.

Cunningham, Patricia M. Phonics *They Use: Words for Reading and Writing*. New York: Longman, 2000.

Forte, Imogene. *Language Literacy Lessons: (Series)* Nashville: Incentive Publications, 2002.

Forte, Imogene. *Lecciones de Lenguaje: (Series)* Nashville: Incentive Publications, 2002.

Forte, Imogene and Marjorie Frank. *If You're Trying to Get Better Grades and Higher Test Scores in Reading and Language, You've Gotta Have This Book!* Nashville: Incentive Publications, 2002.

Forte, Imogene and Sandra Schurr. *Standards-Based Graphic Organizers, Rubrics, and Writing Prompts for Middle Grades Students in Language Arts, Math, Science, and Social Studies.* Nashville: Incentive Publications, 2003.

Frender, Gloria. *Learning to Learn: Strengthening Study Skills and Brain Power*. Nashville: Incentive Publications, 1990.

Gregory, Gayle and Carolyn Chapman. *Differentiated Instructional Strategies: One Size Doesn't Fit All*. Thousand Oaks, CA: Corwin Press, 2002.

Hollimon, L. *The Complete Guide to Classroom Centers*. Creative Teaching Press, Inc. Cypress, CA: Creative Teaching Press, 1996.

Jensen, Eric. *Teaching with the Brain in Mind*. Alexandria, VA: Association for Supervision and Curriculum Development, 1998.

BIBLIOGRAPHY

Marzano, Robert, Debra Pickering, and Jane Pollock. *Classroom Instruction That Works*. Alexandria, VA: Association for Supervision and Curriculum Development, 2001.

Moore, David, John Readence, and Robert Rickelman. *Pre-reading Activities for Content Area Reading and Learning*. Newark, DE: International Reading Association, 2000.

Nagy, William. *Teaching Vocabulary to Improve Reading Comprehension*. Newark, DE: International Reading Association, 1988.

National Reading Panel. *Teaching Children to Read: Report of the Subgroups. Report to the National Reading Panel*. Washington, DC: National Institute of Child Health and Human Development, 2000.

The Partnership for Reading: National Institute for Literacy, National Institute of Child Health and Human Development, and U.S. Department of Education. Put Reading First: The Research Building Blocks for Teaching Children to Read. Washington, DC: U.S. GPO, 2001.

Pearson, P.D., and Johnson, D.D. *Teaching Reading Comprehension*. New York: Holt, Rinehart and Winston, 1978.

Robb, Laura. *Teaching Reading in Middle School*. New York: Scholastic Professional Books, 2000.

Schwartz, Robert M., and Taffy Raphael. "Concept of Definition: A Key to Improving Students' Vocabulary." *Reading Teacher*, 39 (2) (1985), 198–205.

Shalaway, Linda and Linda Beech. *Learning To Teach . . . Not Just for Beginners*. New York: Scholastic Professional Books, 1998.

Silver, Debbie. *Drumming to the Beat of Different Marchers: Finding the Rhythm for Differentiated Learning*. Nashville: Incentive Publications, 2005.

How to Teach Reading . . .

Snow, Catherine, M. Susan Burns, and Peg Griffin, eds. *Preventing Reading Difficulties in Young Children.* Washington DC: National Academy Press, 1999.

Sousa, David. *How the Brain Learns.* Thousand Oaks, CA: Corwin Press, 2001.

Sousa, David. *How the Brain Learns to Read.* Thousand Oaks, CA: Corwin Press, Inc., 2005.

Stahl, Steven. *Vocabulary Development: From Research to Practice.* vol. 2. Cambridge, MA: Brookline Books, 1999.

Tierney, Robert and John Readence. *Reading Strategies and Practices: A Compendium.* 5th ed. Boston: Allyn and Bacon, 2000.

Tomlinson, Carol Anne. *The Differentiated Classroom: Responding to the Needs of All Learners.* Alexandria, VA: Association for Supervision and Curriculum Development, 1999.

Tovani, Cris. *I Read it, But I Don't Get It: Comprehension Strategies for Adolescent Readers.* Portland, ME: Stenhouse Publishers, 2000.

Vacca, Richard and Jo Anne Vacca. *Content Area Reading.* 4th ed. New York: Harper Collins, 1993.

Walberg, Herbert J. Walberg and Shiow-Ling Tsai, "Matthew Effects in Education," *American Educational Research Journal,* 1983, 20:359-373.

Wolfe, Patricia. *Brain Matters: Translating Research into Classroom Practice.* Alexandria, VA: Association for Supervision and Curriculum Development, 2001.

Wolfe, P. & Nelvills, P. *Building the Reading Brain, PreK-3.* Thousand Oaks, CA: Corwin Press, Inc., 2005